The Case for Socialism

The Case for Socialism

By Alan Maass

Third Edition

Haymarket Books
Chicago, Illinois

The Case for Socialism by Alan Maass was first published as
Why You Should Be a Socialist in 2001 by the International Socialist
Organization.

This updated edition published in 2010 by Haymarket Books.
© 2010 Alan Maass

"Eugene V. Debs and the Idea of Socialism"
© 1999, 2004 Howard Zinn

Haymarket Books
PO Box 180165
Chicago, IL 60618
773-583-7884
www.haymarketbooks.org
info@haymarketbooks.org

Trade distribution:

In the U.S. through Consortium Book
Sales and Distribution, www.cbsd.com

In Canada through Publishers Group Canada, pgcbooks.ca/home.html

In the UK, Turnaround Publisher Services, www.turnaround-uk.com

In Australia, Palgrave Macmillan, www.palgravemacmillan.com.au

All other countries, Publishers Group Worldwide, www.pgw.com

Cover design by Eric Ruder
Cover photo of marchers outside the 2008 Republican National
Convention in Minneapolis/St. Paul, Minnesota. Photo by Eric Ruder,
September 1, 2008.

Printed in Canada by union labor on recycled paper containing
100 percent post-consumer waste in accordance with the guidelines
of the Green Press Initiative, www.greenpressinitiative.org.

ISBN 978-1608460-73-1

Library of Congress Cataloging-in-Publication data is available.

Contents

The Case for Socialism

Not True! ← *An absolute lie!!!*

Capitalism isn't working.

For millions and millions of people, in the United States and around the world, there just isn't any other way to put it. Every day, every week, every month seems to bring more evidence— hunger and poverty getting worse, jobs lost and homes in foreclosure, war and environmental destruction. And all the while, a tiny elite enjoys a life of unbelievable wealth and privilege, completely removed from what the rest of us go through.

This describes Socialism.

The claims made in support of the capitalist system—that if you work hard and sacrifice, you'll be rewarded, you'll get ahead, your children will have better opportunities than you— have been revealed as frauds for the majority of people in society. Instead, it's gotten harder and harder to make ends meet. And if you should have the bad luck to face an accident or unexpected crisis—or if, like so many people in the United States, you were born into poverty and never had a chance to "get ahead" in the first place—then watch out.

1

Ask Evan Gutierrez. In December 2008, he lost his job on the staff of a church and community center in Los Angeles because of cuts in funding connected to the Wall Street financial crisis. He was hired as a music teacher at a charter school, but had only just started when the school shut down. With a child on the way, Evan and his wife moved to a 500-square-foot apartment to save money. They still fell behind on rent, and Evan had to ask for help from the church's goodwill fund that he used to help administer. "We grow up with the impression there's a correlation between effort and the fruits of your labor," he told the *New York Times*. "To be honest with you, I have very little confidence I'm going to be able to turn this around. It just feels completely, completely out of my control."

A few hundred miles north, the Ferrell family is struggling to get by in Lincoln, California. Thankfully, Jeff Ferrell still had his job—as a state worker inspecting workplaces for health hazards—as the holidays approached in 2009. But Governor Arnold Schwarzenegger's budget-cutting government had imposed a two-day-a-month furlough, which added up to a 10 percent pay cut for the Ferrells. Now, before she goes grocery shopping—at the WinCo discount chain—Sharon Ferrell calls her bank's toll-free number to find out how much money is left in their account, and she keeps a calculator in the cart to make sure she doesn't go over. "We've cut the fat all along," she says, "and so this is really pushing us close to the bone now."

Jeff and Sharon must fear that their twin girls will face the same difficulties in a few years that Colleen Riley does now on the other side of the country. Colleen graduated from the University of Rhode Island in May 2009, but the best job she could find was for only twenty hours a week. There was no way for her to keep her apartment—she moved back in with her parents. At the end of the year, still looking for full-time work, she had her first repayment on $10,000 in student loans staring her in the face—along with the loss of health insurance coverage under her parents' policy.

Taking care of his family was the reason Ignacio Sanchez came to the United States from Mexico. He found work as a laborer in New York City, making up to $200 a day sometimes, and he sent home as much as he could. Then the crisis hit, and the jobs dried up. Ignacio, too, could no longer afford the rent. Fearful that the shelters would ask for identification, he and other undocumented workers spend their nights on the streets, often camped out under a train bridge in Queens. "By the railroad tracks, the ground was sprinkled with the instruments of coping: empty beer bottles, a tattered Bible, a crumpled picture of a young boy," the *New York Times* reported. Ignacio summed up his bleak situation: "This is no life."

Stories like these aren't the exception. They can be found in every corner of the United States. They are the grim consequences of an economic crisis that pushed unemployment, poverty, hunger, home foreclosures, health insurance coverage—literally any indicator of working-class living standards you could name—to the worst levels in at least a generation. And with the second decade of the twenty-first century getting under way, most people agreed with Evan Gutierrez that there didn't seem to be much reason to expect better times. For people like

Evan and so many others, the whole system seems to be stacked against them.

No wonder an April 2009 Rasmussen Reports poll found that only a bare majority of Americans believed capitalism was a better system than socialism—and that people under thirty were evenly split in their preference for socialism or capitalism. There's a growing discontent with capitalism and its upside-down priorities, even in the world's richest country, not to mention around the globe. The idea that there ought to be an alternative to the misery and injustice of the world today sounds good to more and more people.

Now, to someone like Glenn Beck, this doesn't sound very good at all. You might even say that it's a specter haunting him. "Socialism," Beck declared on his radio show in January 2009, with that trademark teary quaver in his voice, "doesn't seem to be a bad thing in America anymore. Most people are like, 'Yeah, socialism isn't so bad.'"

Of course, for him and the other ranters of the right wing, the chief evidence that socialism is washing over America was the election of Barack Obama as president. That presents a problem, since Obama is quite insistent that he isn't a social-ist—and he's gone far out of his way to prove it, filling his Treasury Department with refugees from Goldman Sachs, ex-panding U.S. wars, and generally acting like his highest priority is preserving the status quo.

If that were all there was to it, Beck could sleep soundly. But the return of socialism to the political discussion in the United States has deeper sources than the right wing's misplaced fears about Obama. There was the near-implosion of the world financial system at the end of 2008. The federal government's rush, under Bush and Obama alike, to save the bankers with taxpayer money. The ongoing effects of the Great Recession. The disastrous invasion and occupation of Iraq. The Hurricane Katrina nightmare in New Orleans and the attitude of callous contempt it exposed in Washington, D.C. The Christian right's shrill intolerance. And, increasingly, the frustrations with a new president who said one thing on the campaign trail to get people's votes, but is doing another in office.

The certainties of previous decades—that capitalism, whatever its flaws, is the only workable system—have broken down, leaving a sense that something different is badly needed. The question is what that "something different" should be. What is the alternative?

This book proposes socialism. But real socialism. Not the hysterical caricatures of blowhards like Glenn Beck and others on the right. Socialism is also not the former USSR, or any of the remaining outposts of Stalinist totalitarianism, like North Korea or the corporate-friendly, sweatshop haven of China. Nor is it the center-left parties in European countries that call themselves socialist, but govern with pro-capitalist policies little different from their conservative counterparts.

The genuine socialist tradition is fundamentally different from all these. At its heart, socialism is about the creation of a new society, built from the bottom up, through the struggles of ordinary working people against exploitation, oppression, and injustice—one that eliminates profit and power as the prime goals of life, and instead organizes our world around the principles of equality, democracy, and freedom.

The Reverse–Robin Hood Society

We live in a world of shocking inequality. Almost half the world's population—more than three billion people, the equivalent of the population of ten United States—lives on less than $2.50 a day. A billion people are undernourished and go to bed hungry each night. Two in five people around the world lack access to clean water, and one in four lives without basic electricity. Even in the United States, one in five children is born into poverty, and there's a better than even chance that we will spend at least one of our years between the ages of twenty-five and seventy-five below the poverty line.

But amid this crying need, there is immense wealth—fortunes beyond imagining for most people. Just how immense? Think of it this way: Let's say we had a full year's wages for the average U.S. manufacturing worker—$37,107 at the end of 2008, according to the Labor Department—in stacks of $20 bills. If we laid all the bills end to end, they would stretch 928 feet. That's almost one-sixth of a mile—about three-quarters of a lap around a football field.

Now take Microsoft founder Bill Gates. According to *Forbes* magazine's survey of the richest Americans in 2009, he was worth $50 billion. If we had Gates's fortune in $20 bills, laid end to end, they would stretch for 236,742 *miles*. That's one million laps around a football field. Or six laps around the full circumference of the earth.

Bill Gates's fortune would stretch from the earth to the moon.

The ranks of the astronomically rich thinned a bit as a result of the financial crisis that began in 2007. But according to *Forbes*, the world's 793 billionaires as of 2009 still had a combined worth of $2.4 trillion. That's *twice* the combined gross domestic product of all the countries of sub-Saharan Africa, according to the World Bank—and more than the total annual income of the poorest half of the world's population.

Yes, you read that correctly. There are 793 people with more money than three billion people.

What does this tiny elite *do* to have so much more than anyone else? The answer to this question is actually more infuriating.

Let's consider one of them: Stephen Schwarzman, Corporate America's best-paid chief executive in 2008 and number 50 on the *Forbes* 400 list of richest Americans the next year. In 2008, Schwarzman raked in $702 million as head of the Blackstone Group, a Wall Street investment firm—most in the form of stock awards from an arrangement struck before Blackstone became a publicly traded company the year before.

What does Blackstone do that it needs to reward its top executive so handsomely? Blackstone is one of the world's leaders in private equity investments, having helped pioneer the corporate takeover strategy. The idea is that an investment group swoops in and buys control of a company, takes out huge loans to finance the purchase, restructures operations to slash costs and free up cash, then resells the company and pays off the debt, while pocketing a big profit. The basic principle is nothing more than buy low and sell high, but the key is in the borrowing, or what Wall

Street calls leverage. If you can get control of a company by only putting down a fraction of its purchase price, then your rate of return on the original investment multiplies.

Blackstone has diversified into other areas. It dabbles in real estate and manages some hedge funds. But these other operations share something in common with Blackstone's main business: They contribute nothing of any use to the economy or society. Blackstone doesn't launch new businesses or develop innovative products. Its chief activity is to be a traveling parasite. It buys existing companies, sucks money out of them, and gets rid of them, preferably as fast as possible. Firms like Blackstone are the financial equivalent of the Bible's plagues of locusts, descending on areas, stripping them bare, and moving on.

The locust business has been good to Stephen Schwarzman. He lives in splendor in Manhattan in a 35-room triplex on Park Avenue, once owned by John D. Rockefeller, which he bought in May 2000 for $37 million. For weekends, depending on the season, he repairs to his mansion on eight acres in the Hamptons, or the 13,000-square-foot British colonial–style estate on a private spit of land in Palm Beach, Florida. There's also a beachfront mansion in Jamaica, but Schwarzman says he likes to leave that for his children to use.

"I love houses," Schwarzman told a reporter. "I don't know why." Probably the one hundred thousand people estimated to be homeless on an average night in New York City would say the same. But they would know why.

When Schwarzman turned sixty in February 2007, he threw himself a birthday party. Not an ordinary party, of course, but one befitting a man of his grand accomplishments. He rented the cavernous Park Avenue Armory and spent a reported $3 million transforming it into a giant-size replica of his Manhattan luxury apartment. Guests—among them, the governors of New Jersey and New York, foul real estate tycoon Donald Trump, and, naturally, dozens of Schwarzman's fellow Wall Street parasites—dined on lobster, filet mignon, and Baked Alaska, and enjoyed (if such a thing is possible) a private concert by Rod Stewart.

On that one night, Schwarzman blew more money than 163 New York City families living at the poverty line—which is the fate of one in five residents of the city Stephen Schwarzman calls home—will see in a full year.

What could possibly justify this? One man, whose life's work has been to manipulate the labor, property, and wealth of others for his own gain, lives in a world of unimaginable privilege and power, where he can indulge any whim. And all around him is another world in which millions of people will work hard all their lives just to get by, and never accumulate a fraction of what he spends on a birthday party.

This twisted story is repeated throughout a capitalist society. The system that made Stephen Schwarzman a billionaire because of his skills as a financial parasite is the same system that protects his friends on Wall Street with a multi-trillion-dollar government bailout. The system that saves Wall Street from going under is the same system that devotes hundreds of billions of dollars every year to a military machine that goes to war for oil or whatever else serves the interests of the corporate elite.

Sometimes, discussions of wealth and finance can seem otherworldly—sums of money so large that it's hard to wrap your mind around them. But the consequences of capitalism are much more concrete.

The tens of millions that Stephen Schwarzman spent on another mansion in the Hamptons is money that thousands of workers didn't get paid because they were laid off after a corporate takeover engineered by Blackstone. The trillions that the U.S. government committed to the Wall Street banks is money that can't be used to expand food aid programs or to rebuild crumbling schools. The hundreds of billions devoted to the Pentagon every year is money that won't go to conquering AIDS in sub-Saharan Africa.

From the point of view of anyone who wants to do something to make the world a better place, this is money that has been stolen—pure and simple. A great portion of the immense wealth produced around the world is continually robbed to make the rich richer and the powerful more powerful still.

As John Steinbeck wrote in his novel of the depression years, *The Grapes of Wrath*:

> There is a crime here that goes beyond denunciation. There is a sorrow here that weeping cannot symbolize. There is a failure here that topples all our success. The fertile earth, the straight tree rows, the sturdy trunks, and the ripe fruit. And children dying of pellagra must die because a profit cannot be taken from an orange.

The point of socialism, put simply, would be to stop the theft.

Socialism is based on a few straightforward principles. The world's vast resources should be used not to increase the riches of a few parasites, but to eradicate poverty and homelessness and every other form of scarcity forever. Rather than fighting wars that promote the power of the tiny class of rulers at the top, the working majority in society should cooperate in the project of creating a world of plenty. The important decisions shouldn't be left in the hands of people who are either rich or controlled by people who are rich, but should be made by everyone democratically. Instead of a system that crushes our hopes and dreams, we should live in a world where we control our own lives.

The Struggle for a New World

Capitalism is the source of poverty, war, and a host of other evils. But it also produces something else: resistance.

For the last quarter of the twentieth century, the theology of capitalism—with its worship of the free market and demonization of "big government"—reigned supreme in the United States, through Republican and Democratic presidencies. But the economic and political crisis that began during the Bush years and accelerated into the Obama era has exposed the dark side of the system.

The man in Michael Moore's movie *Capitalism: A Love Story* who lost his Illinois farmhouse to foreclosure spoke for many people when he said: "There's got to be some kind of rebellion between people who've got nothing and people who've got it all."

Around the world, this sentiment has been the fuel of social explosions. In Iceland, where the financial crisis became a political one in early 2009, masses of people, braving tear gas and riot police, besieged the world's oldest parliament building, drove the old political establishment from government, and installed a coalition of Left Greens and Social Democrats in power, with the first openly lesbian prime minister in the world at its head. In Bolivia, insurrectionary demonstrations toppled the U.S.-backed government and opened the door to a new stage in the struggle. In Iran, the theft of the presidential election in 2009 sparked mass demonstrations. And these are just a few examples among many.

The United States hasn't see revolts on this scale. But it wasn't quiet either. For example, for millions of people, enthusiasm for Barack Obama's victory in November 2008 was dampened by the success of Proposition 8 in California—a ballot measure that overturned equal marriage rights for same-sex couples. But the passage of Prop 8 set off an explosion of protest, starting the night of the election itself, and building throughout the weeks and months that followed. Rather than react with demoralization, a new generation of activists for LGBT (lesbian, gay, bisexual, and transgender) equality adopted the Obama campaign's message of "Yes we can"—itself appropriated from the immigrant rights movement slogan "Si se puede."

There are other sparks in the air. In California, severe budget cuts ignited a wave of demonstrations in defense of public education as the new school year started in 2009—with students, teachers, faculty, and the community coming together to show opposition. Weeks after the 2008 election, the labor movement was electrified by the factory occupation at Republic Windows & Doors in Chicago, where workers not only succeeded in winning a severance package due to them after being laid off, but also kept their plant open. Sit-ins in Senate committee hearing rooms against the sellout of genuine health care reform. Days of action to stop innocent men from being executed. Civil disobedience against coal companies fouling the Appalachians with mountaintop removal mining.

Such struggles are part of a rich history of opposition to inequality and injustice. And like those of the past, today's movements face a similar message from the powers that be, and also sometimes within their own ranks: Wait. Be patient. Don't be too radical. Be realistic.

Barney Frank seems to have appointed himself spokesperson for these voices in the Obama era. Frank is the veteran congressman from Massachusetts, the first openly gay federal lawmaker, and one of the best-known fixtures of the liberal wing of the Democratic Party. Through the long reign of George W. Bush, he decried the policies of war, scapegoating, and more tax cuts for the already rich. And he spoke passionately about what was needed to end the tyranny of the Republican right: Put the Democrats back in power. Elect a Democratic majority in the houses of Congress. Put a Democrat in the White House.

By Election Day 2008, Frank had his wish. But his passion for change seemed to have cooled. At a 2009 commencement speech at American University in Washington, D.C., Frank advised graduates that "pragmatism," not "idealism" was called for these days. Forget about changing the world. "You will have to satisfy yourselves," he said, "with having made bad situations a little bit better."

It seems fair to ask, though, where "pragmatism" has gotten Barney Frank. As the leading House Democrat shaping Wall Street financial bailout legislation, Frank "pragmatically" engineered the giveaway of hundreds of billions of taxpayer dollars to the banks, while ordinary people losing their homes have nowhere to turn. He "pragmatically" voted for funding the Obama administration's escalation of the war in Afghanistan. Frank "realistically" and "pragmatically" insisted that marriage equality, repeal of the military's "don't ask, don't tell" policy, and every promise that Barack Obama made to LGBT people during the presidential campaign would have to wait.

Ideals, Frank told the American University graduates, "never fed a hungry kid, they never cleaned up a polluted river, they never built a road that got people anywhere … Idealism without pragmatism is just a way to flatter your ego."

Actually, it's the other way around. It's not ideals that never fed a hungry kid. It's being pragmatic that steals the money that could be used to feed hungry children and gives it away to the banks. Pragmatism not only doesn't clean up a polluted river—it fills in the already polluted rivers with the debris of mountaintop mining.

There's an even more important point to be made here. Ideals—the hope that something can be different in society and the determination to act to make it different—are the first ingredient in every great social movement.

If you were Rosa Parks in Montgomery, Alabama, in 1955, and you were ordered to give up your bus seat to a white man, the pragmatic thing to do would be to give it up, wouldn't it?

Because realistically, what can one woman do to stop Jim Crow segregation? But because people like Rosa Parks and thousands of others took action, unpragmatically and unrealistically, they changed history.

The commitment to act—to organize, to agitate and persuade, to petition, to protest, to picket—is the critical first step on the road to change. We live in a world today that badly needs changing, and what we do about it now matters.

CHAPTER ONE

Why Capitalism Doesn't Work

All men are created equal, according to the Declaration of Independence. But when it comes to life, liberty, and the pursuit of happiness, it turns out that—to paraphrase George Orwell's *Animal Farm*—some Americans are more equal than others.

At the end of 2008, with the Wall Street system on the brink of collapse following the bursting of the real estate bubble and the failure of some of the biggest banks in the United States and abroad, Congress and the Bush administration agreed on a $700 billion bailout program to save the financial system. It was an immense sum—about $2,300 for every man, woman, and child in the United States. And that turned out to be only a small fraction of the mind-boggling sums the federal government ultimately put on the line in the rescue.

The Wall Street banks were "too big to fail"—unlike ordinary Americans who run into financial trouble. Millions of people have "bad debts" on their books, and they could be kicked out of their homes as a result. But the federal government is doing next to nothing for them. Under the Obama administration's celebrated Making Home Affordable program, around 30,000 homeowners got their mortgage loans permanently modified as of the end of 2009—about 4 percent of the more than 750,000 people who applied in the hopes that they could avoid foreclosure. In other words, little better than no help at all.

Conservatives say these homeowners brought their problems on themselves. "[F]or every 'predatory lender' out there," lectured right-wing commentator Michelle Malkin, "you can find a predatory borrower … who secured financing and bought a home he knew he couldn't afford with little money down, and bogus or no income verification." Even liberal commentators tend to divide the blame between the financial system for hyping the housing bubble and American consumers for "living beyond their means."

But when you read about the nightmare that took over the final years of Addie Polk's life, it's hard to see her as anything other than a victim—preyed upon by powerful corporate interests that robbed her of one of the only things of value left in her life, and then tossed her aside.

Addie and her husband bought a home in Akron, Ohio, in 1970 and managed to pay it off by 1982, just before they reached retirement age. But during the 2000s, Addie, by then a widow and suffering from a variety of health problems, ran into financial difficulties. So she decided to re-mortgage her home.

The good folks at Countrywide Home Loans were ready to help. At age eighty-six, Addie Polk signed a thirty-year mortgage for $45,620 and took out an $11,380 line of credit. Soon, she began missing payments. In 2007, the government-backed mortgage company Fannie Mae took over the loan and began proceedings to take the house. On October 1, 2008, sheriff's deputies arrived to leave another eviction notice when they heard the gunshots. A neighbor used his ladder to get in a second-floor window, where he found Addie lying unconscious on the bed, shot twice in the chest. She was taken to the hospital, barely alive. Polk died six months later, at the end of March 2009.

Apparently, a ninety-year-old woman's suicide attempt was enough for Fannie Mae—executives found it in their hearts to forgive the loan. But Addie Polk was one among so many. "There's a lot of people like Miss Polk right now," Akron City Council president Marco Sommerville told CNN.

Countrywide Financial, whose home loan division made the new mortgage loan to Addie Polk in 2004, was one among many, too. There were hundreds of mortgage brokers, scores of lenders like Countrywide, banks that bought the mortgages, investment banks that rebought them and sold them again in the form of get-rich-quick investments. They all benefited from encouraging the mortgage boom. There was just so much money to be made off fees, commissions, interest payments, bond sales, portfolio management, and on and on.

Still, Countrywide founder and former CEO Angelo Mozilo stands out as a particularly vile piece of work.

Like any other top executive at a big financial corporation, there were the thousand-dollar suits, palatial homes, and a fleet of Rolls Royces and other luxury cars. Mozilo made a fortune selling his personal stake in Countrywide stock, as the company was headed toward bankruptcy. And when Countrywide got sold off in 2008 to Bank of America, Mozilo had a 24-karat golden parachute waiting—a severance package worth $110 million. Under the glare of publicity, Mozilo gave up some of the deal, but he still got tens of millions of dollars just to walk out the door.

But Mozilo really stood apart because of his unapologetic ruthlessness in victimizing people like Addie Polk. He was the driving force behind Countrywide's meteoric rise to become the country's largest mortgage lender by the 2000s. He pushed the company to steer borrowers toward whatever loans would make the most profit. Countrywide's payment structure made it much more lucrative for brokers to sign up customers for a sub-prime loan than a conventional one. To Mozilo, there was no question that homebuyers should be lured by the promise of low initial payments toward sub-prime mortgages with hidden traps.

Don't expect any humility from the man, now. Mozilo insists that he and his failed company were victims of "economic forces beyond our control." And not faceless economic forces, either. At a conference sponsored by the Milken Institute—named, appropriately enough, after the 1980s junk bond king Michael Milken, who went to jail for financial fraud—Mozilo explained that Countrywide was forced to push risky and highly lucrative sub-prime loans on borrowers because … the loan industry was facing pressure from civil rights advocates to lend more to racial minorities.

Mozilo was at least forced out of the corporate boardroom. But for many of Countrywide's partners in crime, it was nearly business as usual at end-of-year bonus time in 2008, in spite of the near-meltdown on Wall Street and the worst economic crisis since the Great Depression.

The super-bank Citigroup and Merrill Lynch, which was also, like Countrywide, absorbed by Bank of America, lost a combined $55 billion in 2008. But they were among nine major banks that paid out more than $32 billion in bonuses—as they took in a total of $175 billion in government aid, according to an analysis by the office of New York state attorney general Andrew Cuomo. Citigroup and Merrill, despite their catastrophic losses, accounted for more than a quarter of the bonus pool.

Facts like these beg a question: Why did Addie Polk feel like she had no place to turn for help when the U.S. government had billions of dollars to help Citigroup and Bank of America?

There is no other answer but this: Because the free-market system that caused the financial crisis is organized to make sure some people stay rich and get richer while the rest of us pay. Because capitalism is built around the principle that a few people, like Angelo Mozilo, deserve to be rich beyond anyone else's wildest dreams, while others, like Addie Polk—well, their lives and dreams don't count.

The System's Twisted Priorities

Imagine yourself at a casino where you start gambling on games of chance you don't understand, where the rules are being made up on the spot. You bet hundreds of times more money than you have, and then you bet again on the bets. You lose. You're not only broke yourself, but you're taking down other players who let you play with their money—and the casino itself, which didn't ask to see your chips when you started gambling.

You'd consider yourself lucky to stay out of jail, right? Ah, but you aren't a Wall Street executive! In the world of high finance, when you lose, the federal government steps in to guarantee your losses. You get to keep your big salary and bonus. And you're invited to work with the government to cook up the "rescue" program.

This is basically what took place in the financial world during the 1990s and 2000s, when Wall Street witnessed an explosion of high-stakes gambling on immensely complicated financial markets, far removed from the goods-and-services-producing "real economy."

No one asked too many questions because the money was so good—whether you were generating the fodder for the investments by pushing sub-prime mortgages or you were buying the impossibly complex securities, and especially if you were a Wall Street middleman collecting fees from both the buying and selling. When the bubble burst, the whole financial casino went bust. But the main perpetrators on Wall Street—Citigroup, Goldman Sachs, and the rest—were too big to fail, so they got a bailout, courtesy of U.S. taxpayers.

It's easy to get lost in the mind-numbing details of the transactions and the unbelievable greed of the gamblers. But it's worth asking a question that doesn't get raised much: Why did any of this happen in the first place?

No one could possibly claim that the Wall Street financial boom contributed anything to the greater good of society. Even the old standby explanation from Economics 101—that financial markets like the stock exchange help channel money into worthwhile investment opportunities—doesn't wash. The entire world of mortgage-backed securities, collateralized debt obligations, credit default swaps, and everything else concocted by Wall Street in this latest boom was directed toward one thing—making a tiny group of people incredibly rich.

Rolling Stone journalist Matt Taibbi put his finger on Wall Street's general uselessness to society when he compared the banking giant Goldman Sachs to "a great vampire squid wrapped around the face of humanity, relentlessly jamming its blood funnel into anything that smells like money." It's impossible to regard the financial world's binge as anything other than theft—of incomprehensible sums of money that could have been devoted to meeting society's needs the world over.

What's true about Wall Street is true about the capitalist system generally. The free-market system is organized in completely the wrong way for the goal of meeting the needs of the largest number of people in society.

This is obvious if you look at the political issue that came to dominate the first year of Barack Obama's presidency: health care reform. When the Obama administration embarked on discussions about health care legislation, it vowed to work with industry to ensure that a final proposal for "universal health care" represented "all sides." But the problem from the start is the bare fact that the interests of the industry lie in *restricting* health care, not making it universal. So, for insurance companies, the equation is simple—they have to take in more in premiums (and investments on that income) than they pay out in claims. That means their first job isn't to ensure their customers get anything they need, but to limit access to care beyond a level that's profitable.

Likewise, for pharmaceutical companies, the top priority isn't distributing their products to whoever needs them, but to whoever can *pay* for them, one way or another. For example, when Big Pharma—using research developed with government backing—started producing medicines that more effectively combated HIV/AIDS, the drugs didn't get to the poverty-stricken parts of the world where they were needed most because the victims of the disease couldn't afford the companies' extortionate prices. Eventually, the drug giants won an international agreement that protected their patents and profits, in return for wider distribution. Even so, according to a June 2008 United Nations report, 70 percent of AIDS victims around the world have no access to the medicines that could save their lives.

The profit motive of the privatized health care system lies at the root of all the health care horror stories you hear. Like Stacy Grondin, a grocery store manager in Nashville, Tennessee. In 2006, she suffered an episode in which her heart rate spiked. Fearing a heart attack, she went to a hospital emergency room in an ambulance. Problem: Stacy didn't have pre-approval from her insurance company for either the ambulance or an ER visit. She ended up with a $1,000 bill when her claim was denied.

Grondin was still struggling to pay off a medical debt for the care of her nine-year-old daughter Emily, who was severely injured in a 2003 car accident. Emily's father was serving a prison sentence because of that accident, but Stacy was responsible for more than $2,000 in medical costs not covered by her insurance. "When I first saw the bills," Stacy told the *Tennessean* newspaper, "I was kind of mad because I was paying for this insurance which I barely use. Then, when it's needed, it's hardly there."

In terms of technology and resources, the United States has the most advanced health care system in the world. Yet health care is a chronic source of uncertainty for those lucky enough to remain healthy—and a nightmare for those who get sick. Drugs and treatments that could help people live longer, healthier, and more fulfilling lives are often beyond reach because of a bewildering array of restrictions, imposed in the interests of the bottom line.

The health care system illustrates something that's true generally about capitalism: The drive for profit warps every aspect of the system that provides—or doesn't provide—what people need to survive. The failures of the free market aren't an accident but an inevitable result of the thirst for profit.

Think of it this way: In theory, the capitalist free market is supposed to work according to the law of supply and demand, right? The basic idea is that capitalists control what gets produced and how, but they make their decisions according to what people buy. So consumers use their dollars as a sort of "vote," and capitalists compete with each other to provide the products consumers "vote" for.

But there's a problem with the theory: What if you don't have any money? Then you don't get a vote—and capitalists won't produce what you want. In order for the free market to produce what's needed for everyone in society, there would have to be a roughly equal distribution of money to "vote" with. But in the real world, the rich have far more "votes" than anyone else. So the system is bound to put a priority on making products to meet *their* needs.

One result of this is whole industries devoted to products and services that are a total waste. Consider all the money spent on lying—otherwise known as advertising. Few people care all that much about the difference between Sprite and Sierra Mist. But the owners and executives at the companies that produce the two soft drinks do—their profits depend on it. So they spend huge sums trying to convince people to buy one over the other. Companies spent more than $3 million for a 30-second-long commercial during the 2010 Super Bowl. Each ad cost more just to broadcast than a decently paid Teamster driver earns in a lifetime of work delivering products like Sprite.

And advertising is one of the more harmless forms of waste. Governments around the world spend well over $1 trillion every year on their abilities to wage war. The U.S. government's military budget for 2010, including its wars and occupations in the name of "fighting terrorism," was $663.8 billion—almost as much as what the rest of the world combined spends on its armies.

The amounts of money spent on the Pentagon are stunning, but even more obscene is what this spending says about the priorities of the U.S. government. The U.S. nuclear weapons program cost more than $52 billion in 2008, seven-and-a-half times more than the government devoted to the Head Start education program for low-income children and their families. This is two decades *after* the collapse of the former USSR and the end of the Cold War between the two nuclear-armed superpowers. And still, the threat of nuclear annihilation—a war fought with weapons that could destroy the basis of all life—hangs over us.

And the doomsday scenario isn't even limited to war. The everyday workings of the capitalist system are wreaking havoc on the environment—and the first frightening symptoms of a dire future are already present today. Aside from a few "experts" paid off by the energy industry to say otherwise, scientists are virtually unanimous in confirming that pollution from the burning of fossil fuels like coal and oil is leading to global warming. Unless the amount of carbon in the atmosphere is reduced sharply and quickly, the consequences will be drastic—widespread flooding, the spread of tropical diseases, worsening droughts, more severe weather conditions.

Many people believed the new Obama administration—since it actually acknowledges that climate change is taking place, unlike its predecessors—would take strong action on this issue. But the Democrats' first pass at climate legislation was a watered-down half-measure, built around giving polluters the ability to trade their "right" to pollute. Even if the "cap and trade" system works as advertised—and many environmentalists doubt that it will—the resulting reductions in carbon emissions would leave the United States far from what's needed to slow global warming.

The Obama administration's performance at the international climate summit in Copenhagen in December 2009 was even more disappointing. Scientists estimate that carbon emissions by the worst-polluting countries like the United States need to be cut by 40 percent by 2020 to avoid a climate disaster. The Obama team arrived in Copenhagen offering a 4 percent reduction by 2020. The United States worked with Britain to undermine measures to help poorer countries reduce pollution. And when the Copenhagen talks seemed about to fall apart, Obama personally pushed through an "agreement" that scrapped actual targets for cutting emissions.

The U.S. government's behavior in Copenhagen was appalling, but it wasn't alone—every other major government at best fiddled while the world burned. The perverse reality is that each country has to look out for the interests of its own corporations first, so the priority is on blocking any measure that would have a real impact, out of fear that their businesses might lose out. Any rational society would have long ago taken drastic measures to stop global warming from growing worse. But it's profitable to pollute—even when that means the devastation of the environment on a vast and irreversible scale.

This is the madness of the free market. Capitalism does one thing very well—protect and increase the wealth of the people at the top of society in the short term. Meeting the needs of everyone else is secondary, which is why so many people's needs go unmet. From every other point of view—producing enough to go around, protecting the environment, building a society of equality and freedom—the capitalist system is useless.

The Haves and the Have-Nots

Again, none of this is an accident. The lion's share of the U.S. government's discretionary budget is devoted to the military because a small group of people benefit from this setup. Health care is rationed because it's profitable that way for the people who own and control health care companies. Money is plunged into financial speculation rather than productive investments because of the immediate, short-term gain for the tiny minority of people who control the bulk of wealth in a capitalist society.

Whenever socialists make this point, there's a quick answer from defenders of the system—it's all a conspiracy theory. Actually, "conspiracies" are commonplace in Corporate America. Just take a look at the crimes of Bernie Madoff, who was arrested in December 2008 for ripping off investors to the tune of $50 billion or so. Madoff claimed to be investing people's money for them, but in reality, he was operating one of the oldest cons around—a Ponzi scheme. The superprofits his customers were so in love with were the result of Madoff taking money that came in from new investors, and using it to pay off obligations to previous ones.

So conspiracies do take place under capitalism, and they aren't even that uncommon. Nevertheless, capitalism doesn't depend on conspiracies. The crimes of Bernie Madoff might seem far removed from the workings of the rest of the economy, where actual goods and services are produced in factories and offices. But there *is* a parallel: another perfectly legal robbery—less spectacular, but actually more lucrative—that takes place literally billions of times every day around the world.

Under capitalism, the small class of people at the top own and control what Karl Marx called the "means of production"— the factories and offices, the land, the machinery, means of transportation, and everything else needed to make useful products. These owners don't make anything themselves. They hire much larger numbers of people to do the actual work of producing or providing various goods or services. Without the labor of the many, the oil would remain in the ground, the vehicles wouldn't be built, the patients wouldn't be treated—and the wealth of the few wouldn't exist.

For their labor, workers are supposed to get a "fair day's wage for a fair day's work." But there's nothing fair about it. Even workers who are paid relatively well don't get the full value of what they produce. Usually, it's much less, because employers have all the advantages in keeping labor costs down—above all, because they are perfectly within their rights to replace employees with someone who will work for less.

Meanwhile, the employers get to keep what's left over after paying wages and other costs of production. According to economics textbooks, this profit is a just reward for the "risk" taken in making an investment. But there's no check on how big profits can get. So for a company that manages to make a 10 percent profit each year after paying its expenses, its owners make back the full value of their investment in ten years. If they were really being rewarded for "risking" their money, the profits ought to stop at this point, when the capitalists have been fully paid back. But, in fact, the owners are much better off after ten years—they still own their original investment, as well as the return they've accumulated. Are the workers they employ that much better off at the end of ten years? Not by a long shot.

Looking at the workings of the system over time helps uncover a reality that isn't immediately apparent on the surface. The wealth of the small class of people at the top of society—not only the money in their bank accounts, but the factories and land and other assets they possess—aren't the result of anything they necessarily contributed, but of the fact that they *own*. When a Bernie Madoff is exposed, there's always a hue and cry about the immorality of ill-gotten riches. But this obscures the bigger crime at the heart of the system. Capitalism is built around organized theft—the theft of a portion of the value of what workers produce by the people who employ them.

One of the most common arguments in defense of capitalism is that the rich deserve their wealth. Microsoft's Bill Gates, worth $50 billion according to the 2009 *Forbes* magazine list of richest Americans, is a favorite example, perhaps because he actually started the company that made him rich.

It could be asked, though: Is Gates's contribution to humanity so important that he deserves to be two million times richer than anyone else? Surely a couple thousand times more wealth would be reward enough? But when you look a little closer, even that's too generous. Gates's company gained control of a particular kind of computer software—developed by other people, not primarily by him—and successfully marketed it as the boom in personal computers took off in the 1980s. In other words, he got lucky.

And in that way, Gates is connected to rich people who were lucky in a different way. Like Jim Walton. He was lucky enough to be the son of Sam Walton, founder of the Wal-Mart retail chain. And he was even luckier when his father died, leaving him and his brothers and sisters with a fortune. Jim Walton never had to do a day of work in his life. Yet he's worth more money right now than *one million* people making the federal minimum wage will earn, combined, in a year of full-time work.

The truth is that the rich do nothing to deserve having so much more than anyone else. Typically, in fact, they do nothing much at all. They almost never have anything to do with actually making or distributing the products that people buy. Bill Gates doesn't assemble or package or transport or sell Microsoft products. He doesn't even come up with the software. Gates is rich because he's *owns.* He and his fellow Microsoft shareholders own the means of producing computer software—the factories and offices, machines, patents on various technologies. That's the source of their wealth.

Poverty amid Plenty

If it's true that the rich never did anything to deserve to be so much richer than anyone else, then what about the opposite? Did the poor do anything to deserve to be so poor?

Remember Angelo Mozilo, the ex-CEO of Countrywide? Now that he's out of work, he might decide to spend more time at his beach house in Montecito, California, an hour's drive up the Pacific coast from Los Angeles. But if he heads into nearby Santa Barbara for some fine dining, he'll find fewer parking lots for his luxury cars. That's because Santa Barbara, in spite of its reputation as a playground for the elite, has set aside twelve municipal parking lots for a new wave of homeless people who live out of their vehicles.

For three months in 2008, Barbara Harvey was one of the parking lot residents. The 67-year-old former loan processor and mother of three grown children lost her job in 2007. From that point, "[i]t went to hell in a handbasket," she told CNN. Barbara found another job, but part time at $8 an hour wasn't enough to afford rent, even with her Social Security benefits. And so she ended up among Santa Barbara's parking lot homeless. "I didn't think this would happen to me," she said. "It's just something that I don't think people think is going to happen to them ... It happens very quickly, too."

Santa Barbara is only the tip of the iceberg—and an unrepresentative one, in a lot of ways. In the city of Akron, where Addie Polk tried to kill herself rather than be evicted, the neighborhood around her house was filled with people facing similar problems. "Now I'm going to have a house on my left and a house on my right vacant," said Robert Dillon, the 62-year-old neighbor who climbed into Addie's home and found her. "That doesn't make me feel good, because we were good neighbors."

Government statistics revealed a frightening rise in poverty at the end of the 2000s as a consequence of the economic crisis. The number of Americans living below the poverty line—itself set pitifully low, compared to what's needed to survive in the United States—jumped to 39.8 million in 2008, nearly one in every seven Americans, and that was before the economy took its biggest hits in employment and income. Nearly fifty million people—among them, almost one in four children living in the

United States—suffered what the government calls "food insecurity" in 2008, a dramatic 30 percent increase over the year before.

There are plenty of well-fed academics who will tell you why people like Barbara Harvey went through what they did. "If poor people behaved rationally, they would seldom be poor for long in the first place," sniffed New York University political science professor Lawrence Mead in an interview with author Jonathan Kozol. Smug words. But among the millions of people with stories like Barbara's, there is little "irrational" about anything they did. The only irrationality exists in the miserable circumstances they had to deal with in the first place.

What's true about the most vulnerable in society applies more widely. Working-class people live harder and more difficult lives in all kinds of ways, not because of anything they did, but because of what was done *to* them—and what is *still* being done to them.

The U.S. Census Bureau reported that household income, adjusted for inflation, fell by 3.6 percent in 2008. And the statistics for 2009, when they become available at the end of 2010, will be worse—probably a 4.5 to 5 percent drop, according to the Economic Policy Institute. In other words, a nearly 10 percent cut in the living standards of working families in a matter of a few years—far and away the worst decline since statistics on household income started being kept a half century ago.

That's the consequence of the deepest economic crisis since the Great Depression. But also shocking is the fact that these declines come at the end of a decade of stagnating income for the majority of people in U.S. society—even during the years of economic expansion. For the years preceding the big drop of 2008, median family income actually fell by a fraction from 2000 levels—making the 2000s economic expansion the first in history where median income didn't grow.

Instead, all the benefits of the boom went to the tiny handful of people at the top of society. Between 2002 and 2006, while working-class wages were stagnating at best, income for the richest 1 percent of people grew by 11 percent *per year* on average, according to calculations by economist Emmanuel Saez. By the end of this period, the richest 10 percent of Americans pulled in 49.7 percent of total wages, "a level higher than any other year since 1917, [even surpassing] 1928, the peak of the stock market bubble in the 'roaring' 1920s," Saez reports.

This is nothing less than the radical redistribution of wealth from poor and working people to the very richest few—and it has continued and even accelerated under the Obama administration with the bailout of Wall Street.

To pull off a theft on this scale, Corporate America had to exploit every opportunity. Like when the wealthy buyout firm Brynwood Partners took over the cookie maker Stella D'oro and presented the 136 union workers in its New York City factory with a new contract that would have slashed wages by up to 25 percent, made them pay for health care for the first time, frozen pensions, and eliminated holidays, vacations, and sick pay. The Stella D'oro workers went on strike, and after eleven months on the picket line, won a National Labor Relations Board decision that forced the company to back down. But the workers learned after their victorious return that Brynwood would close the factory and move production out of the Bronx rather than honor a new contract.

This kind of scorched-earth assault has been repeated at thousands of workplaces around the country, non-union as well as union. And the same squeeze can be felt in every other aspect of life for ordinary people. Higher education, for example, is rapidly becoming what it was a century ago—a privilege enjoyed by the wealthy. The cost of tuition and fees at U.S. universities increased by 439 percent between 1982 and 2007, while money devoted to financial aid grants dried up. The only option to fill the gap: more student loans. The median debt for students with loans graduating from a four-year private school was nearly $20,000 as of 2006, the College Board reported.

And that's *before* the budget crisis of the state governments really hit. In California, where state political leaders approved budget cuts worth $15.5 billion in July 2009, the Board of Regents for the celebrated University of California system voted to raise undergraduate fees by a stunning 32 percent for the school year starting in fall 2010. K–12 public education was hammered as well. As the school year began in fall 2009, layoffs of teachers in Arizona public schools pushed class sizes as high as 50 students. In Los Angeles high schools, the norm is 42.5 students per teacher.

As of the end of 2009, "27 states had reduced health benefits for low-income children and families; 25 states are cutting aid to K–12 schools and other educational programs; 34 states have cut assistance to state colleges and universities; 26 states have instituted hiring freezes; 13 states have announced lay-offs; and 22 states have reduced state workers' wages," wrote left-wing economist Rick Wolff, quoting a study by the Center for Budget and Policy Priorities.

But amid all the cutbacks, one special interest isn't being asked to sacrifice. You guessed it: Corporate America still enjoys the generous tax breaks and other incentives that local and state governments used to lure them or to convince them to stay put. At the federal level, the portion of revenue coming from corporate taxes has fallen to below 10 percent, down from about 33 percent half a century ago.

Anyone who raises these inconvenient facts in the main-stream political discussion—much less proposes to do something about them—is accused of using the rhetoric of "class war." But the reality is a class war is already being waged—by one side only. Warren Buffett, the world's second-richest man, was at least honest when he said on ABC's *Nightline*: "I'll tell you, if it's class warfare, my class is winning."

What about Buffett, though? He has a reputation as being more liberal and generous than his fellow billionaires. The currency speculator George Soros gives money to social justice causes. Does that mean capitalists can be shamed into doing good? The short answer is no. Individual capitalists may donate money to charity, even ones that do help the poor. But that doesn't change their social and economic role, nor the system as a whole.

In 2006, Buffett promised to donate more than 80 percent of his fortune—after he kicks the bucket—most of it to Bill

Gates's philanthropic foundation. "We're in awe of a Buffett or a Gates," gushed the *Chicago Tribune*'s Julia Keller at the time, "not just because these people made a lot of money, but because they made a lot of money and then turned around and gave a great deal of it away to causes they deemed worthy."

This "awe" is undeserved. Buffett and his class are spectacularly rich—more so in comparison to the rest of us than at any time in nearly a century—because they have been successful in waging a class war, extending from America's workplaces to the Wall Street casino to the halls of government in Washington, D.C. An individual capitalist like Buffett may give a part of his fortune to charity. But any more than a fraction of it, and he risks losing ground to his competitors. Any concession to priorities other than maximizing profit is an advantage for the other guy. In that sense, the members of the capitalist class—whatever their individual philosophies and sympathies—are disciplined by the iron rules of the free market.

It isn't simply the case that some people in the world are rich and some people are poor. Some people in the world are rich *because* other people are poor. People like Warren Buffett are rich *because* people like Barbara Harvey or Addie Polk are driven all their lives to work harder for less, until they're kicked aside. A very small number of people are rich *because* others go hungry, *because* others have nowhere to live, *because* others endure the horrors of war, *because* the future of the environment is put in jeopardy.

If capitalism has a first principle, it isn't to be found in Warren Buffett's professions of sympathy for the have-nots. It comes from Larry Ellison, the megalomaniacal head of the software giant Oracle, and another of the world's richest men. Ellison is known for paraphrasing the thirteenth-century warlord Genghis Khan: "It's not enough that we win; everyone else must lose."

That perfectly captures the dog-eat-dog world of capitalism. Once you strip away the myths and the scapegoating, what remains is a system that is organized to keep the rich rich, and getting richer—at whatever the cost to the rest of humanity. That's why socialists are dedicated to ending inequality—and a radical redistribution of the wealth and power of capitalist society.

CHAPTER TWO

Land of the Not-So-Free

When Barack Obama was inaugurated as president in January 2009, he took the oath of office in front of a Capitol building that was built with slave labor. The Constitution he swore to uphold originally counted Black slaves as three-fifths of a human being. No more than two generations before, Obama might not have been served a cup of coffee in a restaurant blocks away from the Capitol. And far more recently than that, it was considered a political impossibility for an African American to be elected president.

For millions of people, Obama's inauguration represented something historic—a sign of progress over the legacy of discrimination and violence that runs through American history. The sea of people jammed into the Mall area in front of the Capitol was a moving testament to the popular desire to witness this step forward.

So it was galling to hear Obama's inauguration appropriated by right-wing ideologues as evidence for their long-held claim that racism is a thing of the past. Dinesh D'Souza, author of an obnoxious 1995 book *The End of Racism*, said he "felt a sense of vindication … My argument was that racism, which once used to be systematic, had now become episodic. In other words, racism existed, but it no longer controlled the lives of blacks and other minorities."

If D'Souza walked a few miles south and east of the Capitol building—going the other direction from the White House down Pennsylvania Avenue—he would have a hard time selling that fable. In the predominantly Black Anacostia neighborhood, located in the shadows of the most powerful government in the world, half of all children live in poverty, and nearly half of all students will drop out before graduating high school. The average individual annual income is $14,210, roughly one-quarter of the D.C. average.

In the city as a whole, which is majority African American, the employment rate for Black adults fell to about 50 percent during the 2000s. The rate of infection with HIV/AIDS ranks with the Republic of Congo and Rwanda—one in every twenty residents is infected with HIV and one in fifty has AIDS, ten times the national level. Then there are the horror stories of what is laughably called the criminal "justice" system. At the turn of the twenty-first century, half of African American men in D.C. between the ages of eighteen and thrity-five were under the supervision of the criminal justice system—in prison or jail, on probation or parole, out on bond or being sought on a warrant.

Such statistics are nearly as stark elsewhere in the United States. Incredibly, the world's richest country jails more of its population than any other. But even more shocking is the overwhelming disparity when it comes to race: As of 2007, Black men accounted for about one in every seventeen people in the U.S. population, but one in every three inmates in state and federal prisons or jails. Similarly, racial profiling is a fact of life in America. Consider this from a report published by the far-from-radical Rand Corporation think tank: "In 2006, the New York City Police Department stopped a half-million pedestrians for suspected criminal involvement. Raw statistics for these encounters suggest large racial disparities—89 percent of the stops involved nonwhites."

There's more: When the recession of the late 2000s hit, Blacks were—as ever—disproportionately its first victims. By the middle of 2009, the official unemployment rate for African Americans was 15.1 percent, compared to 8.9 percent for whites.

So much for the idea that racism is a thing of the past. Anyone who honestly examines the evidence has to recognize that bigotry and discrimination against Blacks still thrive in America—not as isolated cases caused by the behavior of a few rotten apples, but as something embedded in the fabric of American society.

So Barack Obama's election represents a contradiction. An African American became president of a country built on slavery, but he presides over a society where racism remains deeply entrenched. Obama's success is representative of how a minority of better-off African Americans have seen barriers to their social advance fall and discrimination against them grow less burdensome. But at the same time, conditions for the majority of African Americans—forty years after the civil rights movement—are little improved, if not worse in some ways.

African Americans aren't the only victims of racism, of course. So are Latinos, so often viewed as "illegal" in the eyes of authorities, whether or not they are documented. So are people of Arab descent and Muslims, enduring harassment and violence—and sometimes unjust imprisonment with no legal recourse—because the shade of their skin color brands them as potential terrorists, according to the cheerleaders for war.

Nor are racial, ethnic, and religious minorities the only groups that suffer discrimination and unequal treatment in a capitalist society. Women are actually a slight majority of the U.S. population, but are paid on average 80 percent of what men are for the same work, according to the federal government's own statistics. Women bear a double burden of work inside and outside the home, and they face the humiliations of sexism heaped on them daily by a culture that perpetuates stereotypes. Lesbian, gay, bisexual, and transgender people live in the shadow of violence because of their sexual identity—fear of discrimination and abuse leads many, for at least some period of time, to hide this essential part of themselves.

The list of victims of unfair treatment in this society, based on everything from language to age to physical abilities and more, could go on and on. These are all different forms of oppression—a variety of interlocking ways by which groups of people are discriminated against and kept down, economically, socially, and politically.

These oppressions are a social crime endemic to capitalism, every bit as obscene as hunger or poverty or war. They are too widespread to be aberrations that can be eliminated with better education or a more vigilant legal system. Capitalism depends for its survival on divisions created in the working class, so the struggle for a new society must challenge those divisions.

The Roots of Oppression

When it comes to the conventional wisdom about racism—or any other form of oppression, for that matter—there's more than one fake pearl out there. The racism-is-a-thing-of-the-past claim is popular. But you're just as likely to hear another old chestnut, in some form or another, even though it contradicts the first—that racism and xenophobia are part of human nature, and we'll never get rid of them.

The truth is quite different. Racism is neither a thing of the past nor an inevitable feature of the past, present, and future—and it *does* matter if we do something about it.

Looking at the question historically helps show how racism has endured because of its usefulness to the class of people at the top of society. As Hubert Harrison, a Black American socialist from the early part of the twentieth century, when segregation was the law of the land, explained, "Had [racism] been innate, it would not be necessary to teach it to children by separate schools or to adults by separate [public facilities ... [E]very single fabric in the great wall of segregation which America is so laboriously building is an eloquent argument against the belief that race prejudice is innate."

Racism as we understand it today hasn't existed for longer than five or so centuries. No serious historical account has uncovered a similar form of systematic racial oppression before the dawn of capitalism—with the European conquest of the Americas and the rise of the slave trade, by which Africans were kidnapped and transported in horrific conditions across the ocean to provide cheap labor for a developing agricultural system.

Slavery did exist in different civilizations—most notably, the Roman Empire—but it wasn't based on race. There are examples of xenophobia in some cultures and not in others—but nothing approaching the systematic character of racism under capitalism, with its propagation of a vast and false ideology justifying the inferiority of certain human beings because of their skin color.

That connection to the rise of capitalism isn't coincidental. The need for a controllable pool of cheap labor to work in the fields of the "New World" gave rise to chattel slavery, and slavery required an ideology to help uphold it. As the great Afro-Caribbean Marxist C. L. R. James wrote, "The conception of dividing people by race begins with the slave trade. This thing was so shocking, so opposed to all the conceptions of society which religion and philosophers had ... that the only justification by which humanity could face it was to divide people into races and decide that the Africans were an inferior race."

Capitalism eventually outgrew the need for chattel slavery—in fact, the success of the rising industrial system in the U.S. North depended on capitalists overcoming the political power of the Southern slaveocracy in the Civil War. But as the U.S. economic system was reshaped after the Civil War, the ideology of racism didn't die out—it was adapted to new needs. Sharecropping, with its conditions of near-slavery, thrived, and the South developed an institutionalized system of Jim Crow segregation. In the new circumstances, the ideology of racism continued to provide a means both to justify the fact that one part of the working class was being held down, and to keep workers divided and unable to unite against their common rulers.

In the twentieth century, the civil rights struggle to end segregation ultimately succeeded in establishing legal equality for African Americans. But racism clearly outlived the civil rights revolution in the American South, as we can see—again, both to justify a setup in which one part of the population consistently suffers worse conditions and to block a united resistance.

The same connections between oppression and class interests are clear in the case of the bigotry endured by immigrants in the United States. America has long claimed to be a "melting pot," made up of people of many races and ethnicities, whose ancestors were drawn from the far-flung corners of the world to seek the "American Dream." That's another of the many lies we're taught about the history of this country. For corporations and the U.S. political establishment, immigration has nothing to do with making opportunities available to the world's poor and suffering. Like slavery in an early era, the key is how immigration guarantees a pool of cheap and easily controlled labor.

If you look at the history of the United States, the idea that immigration controls and border security are about keeping immigrant labor out is laughable. For two centuries, one group after another was encouraged to move to the United States under conditions of illegality, and be the scapegoat at the bottom of the heap. Irish, Jews, Germans, Swedes, southern Italians, Eastern Europeans, Asians, Mexicans, Central Americans, Muslims—all have been victims of anti-immigrant bigotry.

Upton Sinclair's famous novel *The Jungle*, about the slaughterhouses of Chicago and the brutal conditions that a succession of immigrant groups suffered around the turn of the twentieth century, captures perfectly how profit and greed drove the system: "Here was a population, low-class and mostly foreign, hanging always on the verge of starvation, and dependent for its opportunities of life upon the whim of men every bit as brutal and unscrupulous as the old-time slave drivers; under such circumstances, immorality was exactly as inevitable, and as prevalent, as it was under the system of chattel slavery."

It's impossible to read these words about Lithuanian meatpackers in Chicago and not think of the conditions endured by immigrants from Mexico and Central America today. They are used twice over—as workers who can be super-exploited because they have no legal rights and as a group that can be pitted against other workers, whether native born or immigrants themselves, to push down the wages of everybody.

The hate directed at immigrants in this society—whether from individual bigots like Lou Dobbs and the Minutemen vigilantes or embodied in anti-immigrant laws at the local, state, and federal level; whether expressed in outright racist slurs or in more loaded arguments about how immigrants "steal" jobs that "belong" by right to native-born workers—serves the interests of those at the top.

The great abolitionist Frederick Douglass, himself escaped from slavery, put it concisely: "They divided both to conquer each."

This isn't to say that economic interests alone shape the different systems of oppressions that operate under capitalism. On the contrary, forms of oppression take on a life of their own, which can sometimes obscure the underlying economic connection. To take one example, anti-immigrant politicians like Tom Tancredo are at odds with sections of Corporate America when they push for strict border enforcement to cut off all immigration. This works against the interests of corporations that depend on a steady, though strictly controlled, supply of immigrant labor. These two positions represent the opposite ends in a spectrum of establishment opinion on immigration. But the spectrum as a whole serves to bolster the system.

In a more general sense, there are obvious differences between the racial oppression suffered by, for example, immigrants in the United States, versus the Black majority under South Africa's apartheid system, versus African Americans in this country. The specific shape of racism in each case causes the victims to experience their oppression differently and—crucially—challenge it in different ways.

These factors are very important to understand. But they shouldn't be a reason to discount the ways that all these strands of oppression are woven into a single fabric—the tapestry of capitalism.

The Struggle for Liberation

Though there's more of a connection than normally acknowledged, different forms of oppression can seem far removed from each other. For example, while there are striking similarities about the pay disparity suffered by women in relation to men and African Americans in relation to whites, other elements of are clearly unique.

Women are primarily responsible for the raising of children and labor inside the family, placing a double burden on them of paid labor at work and unpaid labor at home. Woman and men alike are taught from an early age that this is natural—that women are drawn to the family, instinctively nurturing, deferential, and all the other traits summed up by the cliché "a woman's place is in the home." At the same time, women are taught something else entirely—that their worth depends on the "beauty," their physical appearance, their sexual attractiveness to men (not to other women, of course!).

These contradictory standards for women play out in a particularly toxic way on the issue of reproductive rights, where the current-day attack on women's rights is sharpest. Every survey has shown that women who decide to get and abortion do so overwhelmingly because they can't afford or are unready to raise a child. But to opponents of the right to choose, women who terminate a pregnancy are selfishly thinking of themselves instead of their "unborn children"—and are probably promiscuous to boot. The intent of anti-abortion forces is to harass and intimidate women into staying in their "natural" place. In reality, women can't have real control over any part of their lives if they don't have a choice about their reproductive lives.

A whole ideological haze surrounds women's role in society and the family. If you turn on a television right now, no matter the time of day or night, you'll be bombarded with myths and stereotypes—about women and men. On a sitcom, you'll find the slovenly husband in front the television set and the wife hectoring him to finish that home improvement project. Then come the commercials with women's bodies sexually objectified, used to sell beer or any number of other products. On the cable "news" networks, commentators jabber about the latest carefully "researched" study proving how desperately unhappy women if they try to do anything other than raise children. Then, in the segment, the anchors turn to thinly veiled gossip-mongering about the latest celebrity breakups and breakdowns.

Nothing about this mess of conflicting images and stereotypes truly depicts real women or men—the actual range of their interests and emotions and behaviors, even in a world that tries to get them to conform.

But obscured beneath this tangled overgrowth of ideology is an economic secret at the heart of women's oppression—that critical point unpaid labor in the home. Because women bear the responsibility of raising children and maintaining the family—or to put it in the terms that Karl Marx used, reproducing the next generation of the working class—the capitalist system doesn't have to. Employers are expected to pay wages for people's labor at work—not the full value, of course, but something. But there's no expectation that anyone will provide wages or benefits or anything else for women's labor in the home. That's an immense subsidy to capitalism. In the mid-1990s, the United Nations Development Program estimated that women's unpaid work was worth $11 trillion a year worldwide, and $1.4 trillion in the United States alone.

Once you see this unquestioned aspect of women's oppression, the prevailing ideas about women's role in society suddenly seem ridiculous. For example, why on earth should women make *anything* less than a man doing the same job? The ancient explanations that bolster this inequality are bound up with women's supposedly natural role in the family—the idea that men are the breadwinners and need to be paid more, that women don't remain in the workforce, but move in and out to raise children. That certainly has nothing to do with the realities of twenty-first-century America—where women are the *sole* breadwinners in so many single-parent households, and working outside the home isn't a choice women can freely make, given the deteriorating living conditions for all working-class families.

What basis is there for believing that men are "better suited" for certain jobs, while others are naturally "women's work"? Why should men be the natural breadwinners in a two-person household? What about same-sex couples? Why can't men, in a modern society, be the primary caregivers to children?

Or better yet, why not a social solution? Why should individual families bear the responsibility for raising children, and keeping everyone fed and clothed, with a roof over their head? Why not society as a whole? Imagine a world in which child care was freely available, organized on a neighborhood-by-neighborhood basis, with the state providing whatever financial resources are needed. Imagine a society where you could eat at communal kitchens, again organized at the grassroots level. In those circumstances, the idea that women naturally gravitate to these roles would make as much sense as the ancient belief that the earth was flat and supported on the backs of elephants.

The point of this is to show, first, that the prevailing ideas about women or Blacks or any other oppressed group are designed to bolster a system of oppression—and second, that various forms of oppression can be traced in critical ways to the underlying priorities of an economic system run in the interests of profit and power. If this is true, then the socialist project of creating a new world has to involve all the struggles against oppression in society, and those struggles have to be championed by everyone fighting for socialism.

This view isn't universally accepted, including by people on the left who oppose oppression and would like to see greater equality. Many of them instead emphasize the importance of different movements being autonomous. Socialists believe that the oppressed must have the right to organize in a nay way they see fit—above all, they shouldn't have to wait for others to rally to the cause before they take action themselves. But we also stress what *unites* our side—what connects all the oppressed and exploited, and how we can organize a common struggle.

It's worth pointing out that the other side doesn't worry about transgressing the boundaries of separate political issues.

Consider—if you can bear it—the Tea Partiers promoted by Glenn Beck, Fox News, and the rest of the right-wing blowhards. They happily tolerate racist slurs about Barack Obama in particular and African Americans in general. They want to build a wall on the border to keep out all immigrants, and they think Islam is a threat to national security. They think a woman's place is in the home, that feminism is a crime against nature, and that the church, the state, fathers, husbands—almost everyone except women—should determine what women do with their reproductive lives. They hate LGBT people as much as government-run health care.

Generally speaking, the right doesn't do single-issue politics. They see all their political and social concerns as related to a wider agenda.

Shouldn't our side—those who want to challenge the priorities of a system divided between haves and have-nots—be looking for what unites us in every struggle for justice and freedom? We can be conscious of the specific ways that different oppressions affect various groups differently, while also recognizing that all workers have an interest in seeing every part of the working class succeed in its struggles?

The working-class movement needs to be united to achieve anything. If you look back at the history of the United States, racism against Blacks, discrimination against women, bigotry toward immigrants and more are ever-present. The times when these divisions have been overcome are too few. A movement of the majority of people that doesn't concern itself with the oppression suffered by any person in its ranks—and that doesn't take steps to fight to end those oppressions—is a movement divided against itself.

But a connected point is equally important. Many of the most important working-class struggles of the past were inspired by the example of an oppressed group rising in revolt. Thus, the 1960s civil rights movement trained a whole generation of radicals and inspired millions to protest the Vietnam War and U.S. imperialism. The women's liberation movement took hope from the civil rights struggle. When a struggle for gay liberation broke out in the late 1960s and early 1970s, its first major radical organization called itself the Gay Liberation Front—a conscious reference to the Vietnamese National Liberation Front fighting half a world away for national liberation.

Capitalism needs oppression in all its forms to survive. But as the old slogan of the labor movement puts it, "An injury to one is an injury to all." Therefore, the struggle of one oppressed group for freedom from discrimination and bigotry is the struggle of all.

CHAPTER THREE

The Scourge of War

"Life is returning to normal for the Iraqi people," George W. Bush declared in a radio address in August 2003, five months after the United States invaded Iraq.

But not for Farah Fadhil. A few weeks after Bush's speech, the eighteen-year-old was killed during a U.S. raid on an apartment complex in a town north of Baghdad. It was a slow and agonizing death. Farah's body was cut apart by shrapnel from a grenade tossed by U.S. soldiers. As she lay dying, the soldiers battered their way into her apartment, demanding to know—in English—where the Iraqi guerrilla fighters were hiding. But there was only Farah, bleeding to death on the floor in front of her mother and brother.

Why? Farah's family wanted to know. Did the United States learn that the complex had become, unbeknownst to them, a headquarters for the "Saddam loyalists" resisting Washington's occupation? "All we want are answers," said Qassam Hassan, a neighbor whose brother was killed in the same raid. But there weren't any answers. This story only came to light after a

British journalist from the *Observer* newspaper learned about it from survivors. The Pentagon's press office in Iraq wouldn't even admit that the raid had taken place, much less offer an explanation for why Farah Fadhil had to die.

Her family was left to contemplate the slogans and sound bites that U.S. officials had repeated as justifications for the war since before the March 2003 invasion: weapons of mass destruction, meetings with al-Qaeda, threats to regional stability. They must have wondered: What on earth did that have to do with Farah? A few months later, U.S. soldiers captured their government's one-time ally, now demonized enemy, Saddam Hussein, and the American media once again pumped out the message that Iraqis were better off with the dictator out of power. Not Farah Fadhil, though.

Fast forward six years, and turn 750 miles to the east—to Afghanistan. On May 4, 2009, the residents of Granai and two other villages in the western province of Farah began to relax as dusk fell. Throughout the day, a battle between U.S. forces and Taliban fighters raged around them. The shooting stopped after the Taliban withdrew, though—the men in Granai even attended evening prayers around 7 p.m.

An hour later, the U.S. warplanes struck—dropping weapons so destructive that the victims were torn to pieces, leaving survivors to collect only parts of their remains for burial, according to a *New York Times* report based on eyewitness accounts. Twelve-year-old Tillah was with her mother and two sisters when the attack came. They raced with other villagers to one of the few solid structures in Granai, a seven-room house. The bombardment continued, but Tillah said she felt safe and fell asleep. She woke to the buzzing noise of a plane—and then a huge explosion as another U.S. bomb collapsed the building on the dozens of people huddled for safety inside.

Only one woman and six children emerged from the house alive, the *Times* reported. Tillah herself remembers nothing until she was pulled from the rubble the next morning, suffering from severe burns and injuries. According to the survivors' list of the victims in the three villages, 147 people died.

Six years later, a different U.S. war—and the same question: Why? Why did the U.S. military aim its deadly arsenal at a quiet and sparsely populated village, hours after the fighters it claimed to be targeting had retreated?

This time, there were answers—but none of them honest. At first, U.S. military officials claimed that the Taliban had caused the deaths with a grenade attack designed to look like a U.S. air strike. "We all know that the Taliban use civilian casualties and sometimes create them," said Defense Secretary Robert Gates. The Pentagon finally did admit that American bombs caused the massacre, but said that the death toll was inflated—an official military investigation concluded that only "approximately 26" civilians were killed. As for the twenty-six, military spokesperson Lieutenant Commander Christine Sidenstricker didn't want anyone blaming the United States. "The fact remains," she told a reporter, "that civilians were killed because the Taliban deliberately caused it to happen." Translation: No matter what the United States does, the Taliban is to blame.

So when the survivors of the massacre in Granai ask why their sons and daughters and fathers and mothers are dead, they get the same fraudulent answers that Iraqis got.

This time, though, the answers come from the mouth of a U.S. president that many people hoped would end America's occupations. At a December 2009 speech at West Point to announce a new escalation in the U.S. war on Afghanistan, Barack Obama sounded like he was channeling George Bush when he claimed that "America, our allies and the world were acting as one to destroy al-Qaeda's terrorist network, and to protect our common security … Our overarching goal remains the same: to disrupt, dismantle and defeat al-Qaeda in Afghanistan and Pakistan, and to prevent its capacity to threaten America and our allies in the future."

As a candidate for president the year before, Obama regularly denounced the Bush administration's campaign of lies that portrayed Iraq as bristling with weapons aimed at the United States and its allies, and a home base for Osama bin Laden and al-Qaeda. But the same things could be said about Afghanistan. The main victims of the war have been impoverished people without the slightest connection to bin Laden—people who are as likely to loath the Taliban, the former ruling party, though maybe not as much as they hate American occupation forces that drop bombs on their wedding parties.

The idea that the United States is sending troops to Afghanistan to combat terrorism or help a struggling people is no more true than it was about Iraq. Like Bush before him, Obama's policy is shaped by the interests of the U.S. corporate and political establishment in defending and expanding an American empire around the world. That's why there's been so much continuity in America's war policy with a Democrat in the White House.

Obama did, in fact, promise as a candidate that he would send more soldiers to Afghanistan—the "real war," he claimed on the campaign trail, as opposed to the "distraction" of Iraq. But he's delivered on a scale that must come as a surprise to people who saw him as the antiwar candidate. In his first year in the White House, Obama announced two major escalations that together double the U.S. troop presence. As independent journalist Jeremy Scahill reported, the Pentagon's policy of using contractors to run its occupations expanded under Obama—as of the end of 2009, contractors accounted for two-thirds of the 189,000-strong U.S. military force in Afghanistan. Also on the rise under Obama were attacks across Afghanistan's border into Pakistan by unmanned aircraft, threatening to spread the war still further.

As for the "distraction" of Iraq, it will continue to "distract" for years to come. The Obama administration's promised plan for "withdrawal" will leave as many as fifty thousand troops in the country by the end of 2010—and it *increased* the number of U.S. mercenaries by almost a quarter.

During the Bush years, the United States carried out its agenda in the Middle East in close coordination with Israel— for example, encouraging Israel's war on Lebanon in 2006 that forced a quarter of the population to flee their homes. Obama visited Israel as a senator and declared his solidarity with the Israeli settlers living along the fortified border with Lebanon. When Israel carried out a barbaric assault on the Palestinians of Gaza—explicitly timed for the weeks before Obama's inauguration in January 2009—the president-to-be was criminally silent. Since taking office, Obama's few timid criticisms of settlement construction were ignored by Israel—and Obama, like his predecessors, said nothing more. The result is that Israel remains a militarized outpost in the Middle East, acting in alliance with the United States—while Palestinians languish in the West Bank and the giant open-air prison of Gaza.

All in all, there have been some tactical shifts and rhetorical differences from the Bush years, but the underlying substance of the Obama administration's foreign policy reflects the same bipartisan consensus that has existed for decades. Under Republicans and Democrats alike, the "war on terror" has been an all-purpose justification for expanding U.S. military power abroad and shredding civil liberties at home.

Afghanistan and Iraq have been turned into living hells. In Afghanistan, the Pentagon unleashed the world's deadliest arsenal against a poverty-stricken country already devastated by two decades of warfare. As of 2008, life expectancy in that country was a mere forty-four years. Afghanistan ranks second-worst in the world in child mortality—more than one in four children die before they reach their fifth birthday. The government of President Hamid Karzai, installed by the United States, is utterly corrupt. In the 2009 presidential election that Karzai won by a "landslide," observers estimated that one million ballots cast for him were fraudulent. Karzai's regime depends on the country's most ruthless warlords, whose crimes include forcing women to endure oppressive conditions that differ not at all from those under the Taliban.

The situation in Iraq is equally horrifying. The United Nations High Commissioner for Refugees estimated that more than 4.7 million Iraqis were displaced after the 2003 invasion—about one in five people from Iraq's 2003 population of twenty-five million. Researchers for the *Lancet* medical journal calculated the Iraqi death toll from war at 655,000 as of the end of June 2006—and with a sectarian civil war still raging at that point, the figures today are no doubt higher than one million.

And for what? Stopping terrorism? Avenging September 11? Ridding the world of weapons of mass destruction? Promoting democracy? Freeing women from the burqa? Many U.S. soldiers, who were promised that they would be welcomed as liberators, but instead became cannon fodder, reached their own conclusions. As Tim Predmore—at the time, a soldier on active duty with the 101st Airborne and stationed in Iraq—wrote in an article for his hometown newspaper:

> This looks like a modern-day crusade not to free an oppressed people or to rid the world of a demonic dictator relentless in his pursuit of conquest and domination, but a crusade to control another nation's natural resource. At least for us here, oil seems to be the reason for our presence ... I can no longer justify my service for what I believe to be half-truths and bold lies. My time is done, as well as that of many others with whom I serve. We have all faced death here without reason or justification.

"A Muscle-man for Big Business"

Every American war has been accompanied by a propaganda campaign to justify it. But when you look beneath the surface, the motives of the U.S. government in military conflicts are that plain—and have been since the United States emerged as a world power a century ago with its victory over Spain in the Spanish-American War. Even then, war supporters talked about liberating the subjects of Spain's colonial domination in the Caribbean and the Pacific. But the real aim of the United States was to be the new colonial boss—which is what it became in the former Spanish possessions of Cuba, Puerto Rico, the Philippines, and Guam.

The United States was late among the world's main powers in starting an empire, but it made up for that in violence. It started out in its own "backyard" of Latin America. Over the last century, U.S. troops have invaded Cuba five times, Honduras four times, Panama four times, the Dominican Republic twice, Haiti twice, Nicaragua twice, and Grenada once.

Eventually, American troops spread out around the world—conquering less powerful nations but also fighting with other powerful countries over which would control what parts of the globe. The conflicts were both economic and military, but these empire-building—or imperialist—adventures never had anything to do with democracy and freedom. Countries like the United States don't go to war to stop tyrants or any of the "humanitarian" reasons that politicians talk about. They go to war to preserve and expand their economic and political power.

General Smedley Butler's beat was Latin America. As a Marine Corps officer in the opening decades of the twentieth century, he headed a number of U.S. military interventions, and he was under no illusion about what he was doing:

I spent most of my time being a high-class muscle-man for

Big Business, for Wall Street and for the Bankers. In short, I was a racketeer for capitalism ... Thus, I helped make Mexico and especially Tampico safe for American oil interests in 1914. I helped make Haiti and Cuba a decent place for the National City Bank to collect revenues in ... I helped purify Nicaragua for the international banking house of Brown Brothers in 1909–1912. I brought light to the Dominican Republic for American sugar interests in 1916. I helped make Honduras "right" for American fruit companies in 1903.

U.S. imperialism is no more kindly or charitable today. Socialists are accused of being "knee-jerk" opponents of U.S. imperialism. And we are—because we believe that the U.S. government will never act in the interests of justice and democracy. We believe that it's up to the people of Afghanistan, Iraq, the Middle East, and elsewhere to settle accounts with their local rulers and determine their own fates, free from the meddling of the "great powers."

Many people who were against the Iraq war under Bush— including leading voices of the antiwar movement—are more forgiving when it comes to Obama. They ought to look more closely at this bipartisan history of U.S. imperialism. As Anthony Arnove, author of *Iraq: The Logic of Withdrawal*, put it in an interview with SocialistWorker.org, "It's important to get past the very short-term framework that not just the establishment media but so much of the left has in this country. Essentially, during the Bush administration, whole sections of the left acted as if empire began with George W. Bush—as if it was something managed only by a handful of people: George Bush, Dick Cheney, Donald Rumsfeld, sections of the neoconservative movement, perhaps even the Republican Party more generally."

The U.S. government before Bush Jr. wasn't more "peaceful" or less committed to using military force to maintain U.S. power. For more than a half century, not one day passed in which the U.S. government didn't have military forces committed around the world in one conflict or another. The difference between presidents—Republican and Democrat alike—has been a matter of tactics, and sometimes not even that.

We live in a world of wars, and the U.S. government has had a hand—directly or indirectly, openly or covertly—in stoking most of them, sometimes supplying advice, sometimes the guns, sometimes the soldiers. When weaker countries step out of line—by threatening a vital economic interest like Middle East oil, or jeopardizing the political balance of power in an important region, such as the Balkans in southeastern Europe in the 1990s—the United States and the world's other major powers will try to impose their domination. But the twentieth century also saw two horrific world wars, not to mention smaller conflicts, that were battles *between* the major powers. At their root, these wars were about economic power—about which imperialist country would dominate which areas of the globe.

Wars are a constant feature in the history of capitalism. They are the product of the ruthless competition for profit at the heart of the free-market system—of economic competition between capitalists growing into political and military competition between countries. That's why wars are inevitable under capitalism. Inevitable, that is, unless ordinary people stand up against the violence and a system that breeds war.

McDonald's and McDonnell Douglas

Guns and bombs are only one part of what socialists call "imperialism." The other side of the U.S. government's military reach into every corner of the globe is its domination—along with a handful of other powerful governments—of the world economic system. The two things go together, as *New York Times* columnist Thomas Friedman observed in 1998: "The hidden hand of the market will never work without a hidden fist. McDonald's cannot flourish without McDonnell Douglas, the designer of the F-15, and the hidden fist that keeps the world safe for Silicon Valley's technology is called the U.S. Army, Air Force, Navy and Marine Corps."

The International Monetary Fund (IMF) and World Bank are international financial institutions set up by the United States to control whether poor countries receive desperately needed economic aid. As a result, they can exercise a blackmailer's power to demand government policies that they consider "appropriate." Though they were thrust into the background by the economic crisis of the late 2000s, the IMF and World Bank have a long record of imposing what they called "structural adjustment" on poor countries around the world, forcing governments to slash government spending and sell off state-run companies and services to private buyers whose chief aim is wringing a profit out of them.

This was all part of the era of "neoliberalism," as it became known—of letting the free market rule, which meant the unchallenged domination of the world's biggest economies, especially the United States.

A couple decades ago, it might have seemed like the worst flash points of poverty were in remote regions untouched by the modern economy. That isn't the case today. As a consequence of neoliberalism, it's not unusual in even the poorest countries of central Africa to find modern factories built by Western corporations sitting side by side with shantytowns because the jobs in the factories don't pay a living wage.

This is characteristic of how capitalism has produced more misery and suffering around the globe. But nothing exposes the barbarism of imperialism and the free-market system more clearly than the production of the most basic of all necessities—food—and its use as a weapon by the U.S. government.

Year after year, the United Nations food agency presents the same grim statistic—somewhere around six million children under the age of five will die in the next twelve months because of malnutrition and its related diseases. The number six million has a terrible significance in the modern world—that is the number of Jews murdered by Germany's Nazis in the Holocaust during the Second World War. A holocaust of the world's children takes place every year, because of hunger—and the world's governments fail to act.

Even conservative estimates calculate that enough food is produced around the globe for everyone in the world to get 2,800 calories a day, well above the minimum standard set by the UN Food and Agriculture Organization. And this is food that already exists. According to one study, if the useable land of the world were cultivated effectively, the earth could feed more than forty billion people—far more than are ever likely to inhabit the planet.

But the food doesn't get to the people who need it. More than one billion people—almost one in every six people on the planet—suffered from hunger in 2009, according to the UN. Why? The obscene reason was summarized once by none other than the establishment *Financial Times* newspaper: "People are not hungry these days because food supplies are not available. They are hungry because they are poor." In a capitalist system, food is treated like any other commodity, from cars and televisions to pharmaceuticals and health care. Instead of being organized to feed the hungry, the system is organized around *not* feeding everyone—so prices, and therefore profits, stay high.

In fact, the agribusiness giants have conspired with governments around the advanced world to make sure that prices stay up. Since 2000, the U.S. government has spent between $15 billion and $35 billion every year on direct and indirect agricultural subsidies. Most of the money was used to prop up the price of grains and other crops by buying up "surplus" food. For example, U.S. farmers produce twice as much wheat as the U.S. market needs. This oversupply should cause the price of bread and other products to fall. But the government buys the excess to keep prices up.

The politicians claim that agricultural subsidies support "family farms" in the United States. That's a myth. According to the Environmental Working Group, 71 percent of farm subsidies since 1995 have gone to the top 10 percent of U.S. producers— the biggest agriculture operations, backed, if not owned outright, by multinational corporations.

Much of the food that the U.S. government buys is distributed around the world in the form of food aid. But like everything else it does, Washington's motives aren't pure. U.S. food aid is used as a weapon to promote U.S. interests—both politically, by providing aid where it will help the geopolitical schemes of the U.S. government, and economically, where it will help pump up the profits of American corporations.

U.S. laws require that government food aid be distributed in the form of U.S.-grown products—even when those products exist in abundance in the country they are being sent to. Thus, in the early years of the 2000s, the United States sent more than one million metric tons of grain to the famine-plagued country of Ethiopia—even though Ethiopian farmers estimated that they had at least 100,000 metric tons of locally grown corn, wheat, sorghum, and beans stored in warehouses, which Ethiopians didn't have the money to buy.

Rather than feeding the hungry and helping countries struck by famine to develop agricultural production on their own, food aid from the U.S. government is mainly organized to help U.S. food bosses get rid of "surplus" food that might push down prices and profits. The effect is to keep food prices high at home and undercut competitors abroad, especially in developing countries—while the world's poor go hungry. The German poet Bertolt Brecht might have had this system in mind when he wrote: "Famines do not simply occur—they are organized by the grain trade."

These are the grim conditions of war, poverty, and imperialist domination around the world. But they have sparked a growing resistance—most obviously, in Latin America.

The shift to the left in what the U.S. government has traditionally considered its "backyard" began with the election victory of Hugo Chávez in Venezuela in 1999. In Brazil, Luis Inácio Lula da Silva, a former metalworker, union leader, and head of the Workers Party, seemed a continuation of this trend when he won the presidency in 2002. Lula disappointed his left-wing supporters by embracing many of the neoliberal policies of his predecessors and staking out a role as a sub-imperial power in the region, working closely with the United States. But the tide of struggle continued across the continent, sweeping to power Evo Morales in Bolivia, Rafael Correa in Ecuador, and Fernando Lugo in Paraguay.

In Bolivia, Morales's election was preceded by popular near-insurrections that forced President Carlos Mesa out of office and stopped two other U.S.-backed free-market conservatives from assuming power. The struggle continues under Morales, with the left both criticizing the president's concessions to multinational corporate interests and defending him from a nonstop attack by the forces of the old elite.

The epicenter of Latin America's left turn, however, is Venezuela. Hugo Chávez has declared himself in favor of "socialism for the twenty-first century" and devoted government resources to backing popular organizations and social projects such as mass literacy campaigns. Chávez avoided the fate of other left-wing leaders in Latin America in 2002 when masses of poor Venezuelans descended on Caracas to foil a U.S.-backed coup that had already forced him out of the country on a military transport plane. The coup-makers caved, and Chávez returned to the capital in triumph.

Chávez has championed social reforms and institutions of popular power, including the nationalization of some factories under the control of workers. He has also tried to concentrate political power in his hands and those of an increasingly powerful circle of politicians and functionaries. Chávez is a genuine left-wing opponent of U.S. power in the region and the country's traditional wealthy elite, but he has stopped short of committing himself to mass popular power and democracy. Nevertheless, his rise to power and spreading influence are signals that the era of neoliberalism, presided over by the all-powerful American government, is over—and that millions of people are ready to fight against any attempt to reimpose that domination. The stage is set for more conflicts and struggles to come.

CHAPTER FOUR

What Is the Socialist Alternative?

Socialism is based on a simple idea—that the resources of society should be used to meet people's needs. We should use the tremendous achievements of human beings in every realm of life not to make a few people rich and powerful, but to make sure every person in society has everything they need to lead rich and fulfilling lives, free from poverty, oppression, and violence.

It seems so obvious—if people are hungry, they should be fed. If people are homeless, we should build homes for them. If people are sick, all the advances in medical technology should be available to them. Why on earth should we tolerate a system like capitalism that does the opposite?

To begin with, a socialist society would take the immense wealth of the rich and use it to meet the basic needs of everyone in society. In 2008, the director general of the UN's Food and Agriculture Organization appealed to world governments to devote $30 billion a year to a campaign to end world hunger. The fortunes of Bill Gates, Warren Buffett, Larry Ellison, and a few Walton heirs would cover the tab for most of the next decade. At the Copenhagen climate summit in 2009, the Group of 77 poor countries that will face the worst effects of global warming begged in vain for $200 billion for projects to help them deal with the crisis. If we took back the bonuses paid to employees at the top twenty-three investment banks, hedge funds, and other Wall Street firms, just for 2009, we'd be three-quarters of the way there.

Next, all the money wasted on weapons and war could be spent on something useful. The 2010 federal budget devotes $663.8 billion to the Pentagon and its "overseas contingency operations." For just 6 percent of one year's spending on weapons, we could hire a million new teachers at the current median salary. For less than half of the military budget, we could double the number of teachers at every level of the U.S. education system, and make our schools the engine of a technological, cultural, and artistic renaissance. Cut the $125 billion devoted to major weapons programs, and you could double the budget of the Department of Transportation and start doing something about the scandalous state of public transit systems in U.S. cities.

That's just military waste. How about we abolish advertising? There's all the money spent on buying airtime for commercials to start with. But beyond that, imagine what all the people employed today to peddle McDonald's burgers and Miller Genuine Draft could do if they were asked to use their talents to educate people—about what the government is up to or critical scientific questions like nutrition.

Socialists don't have a blueprint for exactly what a socialist society will look like, because we believe it will be up to the generations who live in one to figure that out. But quite a lot is obvious. Such a society would begin by guaranteeing that everyone has enough to eat and a sturdy roof over their heads. The education system would be made free, from pre-Kindergarten to university graduate programs. Teachers and students could decide how to reorganize the system so school is about what they care about—with the goal of encouraging every child's talents. Health care would be made free and accessible, starting with a network of well-equipped clinics and medical facilities in every neighborhood. No more bills for gas, electric, and other utilities. Public transportation could be made free—and a far better funded and more efficient system it would be.

That's just the beginning. It wouldn't all happen overnight. But if these goals became the top priorities of society, we could trust that people would do everything to make them happen as soon as possible.

Planning Versus the Free Market

A socialist society would not only take away the existing wealth of the ruling class, but also its economic control over the world. The means of production would be owned and controlled by all of society. Everyone would share in the important economic decisions for society.

Under capitalism, the overall direction of the economy is unplanned. Businesses make their investment decisions behind closed doors, in the hopes of getting a leg up on the competition—introducing the year's most popular model, the new product, the next trend. Success means a greater share of the market, more sales, and more profits. So how much food should be produced overall, how many homes to build, what kind of drugs get researched and manufactured, how electricity should be generated—everything is left to the chaos of the free market.

In economic good times, success seems contagious. Companies make ambitious investments and watch the money roll in. Their executives are toasted in the pages of *Forbes* and *Fortune* for their uncanny foresight. Eventually, though, when enough companies jump in, the market gets saturated, and profit rates start to sink. The investment binge of the preceding period goes into reverse.

This, in short, is the boom-slump cycle of capitalism. We're encouraged to think that economic recessions are just the way things are—"something known as hard times," socialist Upton Sinclair once wrote, "a natural phenomenon like winter itself, mysterious, universal, cruel."

But there's nothing "natural" or "mysterious" about economic crises under capitalism. As Karl Marx and Frederick Engels observed, the headlong expansion of capitalism during economic booms lays the basis for slumps to come, because capitalists eventually produce more products than they can sell at an acceptable rate of profit. When profits begin to fall, companies rush to cut costs—and that means cutbacks, layoffs, and factory closures. As Marx and Engels wrote in *The Communist Manifesto:*

> In these crises, there breaks out an epidemic that, in all earlier epochs, would have seemed an absurdity—the epidemic of

> overproduction. Society suddenly finds itself put back into a
> state of momentary barbarism; it appears as if a famine, a uni-
> versal war of devastation had cut off the supply of every means
> of subsistence; industry and commerce seem to be destroyed.
> And why? Because there is too much civilization, too much
> means of subsistence, too much industry, too much commerce.

The idea of "overproduction" is hard to deal with. Most people's experience of an economic crisis is that they can't get
enough of the things they need. If people are homeless on the
streets of New York City, then how can there be "too much supply" of apartments and "too little demand" to fill vacancies? But
from the standpoint of Corporate America, it *is* possible for
there to be "too much supply," even when people go without—
because there's "too much supply" to sell their products for a
decent profit, and that's what matters.

The elementary point of socialism will be to take profit out of
the equation. Therefore, the resources of society could be commonly owned and controlled by everyone, with decisions made
democratically according to what's needed and wanted, not how
much money can be made. Instead of decisions about the economy being left to a few unaccountable people in corporate board-
rooms, a socialist society would be one where priorities and how
to implement them are discussed, debated, and planned by all.

How? To begin with, all workers would have a voice in what
they do at their workplace, rather than management dictating
what takes place. Larger bodies of democratically elected representatives could have a discussion about overall social priorities. The key would be a system that holds the representatives
accountable to the decisions of the people who elected them.

Beyond this, it's worth pointing out that technological advances like the Internet have made it far easier to spread news, information, and a discussion of political and social questions to every corner of the globe.

What Socialism Isn't

Is it possible for everyone in society to share in decisions about society's direction? They have to, if socialist planning is going to work—which is why a socialist society must be democratic. But democratic in a much more profound way than the current system.

Though we hear it all the time, it simply isn't true that democracy and capitalism go hand in hand. Many of the models of the free market in the less-developed world are run by dictatorships. Even in societies that brag about being democratic, democracy is limited to electing representatives every two or four years. Socialism will be far more democratic than capitalism.

For most people, this seems to contradict what they're taught about socialism. The record of the former USSR under Joseph Stalin's rule, as well as China and other so-called socialist countries existing to this day, seems to show that socialism is a top-down society run by party bosses, with the secret police or army on hand to keep people in line.

The truth of the matter is that none of these countries are socialist by the standards of the founders of the socialist tradition—summed up by Karl Marx this way: "The emancipation of the working classes must be conquered by the working classes themselves."

It doesn't matter what the rulers of the ex-USSR and other so-called socialist countries described themselves—any more than it matters to our understanding of "democracy" that the Democratic Party in the United States was the party of Southern slave-owners before the Civil War and Dixiecrat segregationists after. The question is whether workers control society. In the USSR and other bastions of "socialism," the experience of workers wasn't one of freedom and democracy but of exploitation, oppression, and alienation from any kind of social and political power.

The state did own the means of production in the USSR. But the real question is: Who owns the state? If the answer is anything other than the mass of people, exercising their "ownership" through some system of grassroots democracy—if there is an elite, however well- or ill-intentioned, exercising power over how society is run—then that's a society that violates the most basic definition of socialism.

Other countries are routinely misidentified as socialist, as well—most commonly, European nations with a highly developed social welfare system, such as Sweden. Though their "socialist" characteristics have been hollowed out in the era of neoliberalism, these countries do, in fact, boast better conditions for working people because of the central role of the state in providing a social safety net. But do working-class people exercise any real control in such societies—or are they subordinate to the decisions made above them?

When you strip away the words that the rulers of any of these societies use to describe themselves, what you find are systems that have features similar to capitalism as we know it in the United States. Above all, you find a small minority that exercises preemptive control over what happens in society, and that enjoys greater privileges and power.

This is most clear in the European countries commonly associated with socialism. After all, if state ownership of industry were the sole defining characteristic of a socialist society, we'd have to say that Margaret Thatcher—the Ronald Reagan of Britain—was at least partly a socialist, since her government did own Britain's coal industry (long enough to wage war on the miners' union) and the National Health Service.

The same point applies to the ruling bureaucracy in the former USSR under Stalin and those who followed him. This ruling class, like its counterparts in Western-style capitalism, organized production to meet the demands of competition—not the economic competition of individual capitalists fighting to dominate the market, but the military competition of state capitals fighting for political survival. As under capitalism in the West, the goal was to squeeze as much as possible out of the workforce—in Stalinist Russia's case, machinery and factories that could be devoted to military production. When you think about the insane race to accumulate the means to destroy the planet during the Cold War with the United States, you can see very clearly how the logic of capitalist production could apply under the rule of the "Marxist" bureaucracy in the ex-USSR.

Likewise with countries where the "socialist" rulers aren't so obviously exploiters and oppressors. For example, Cuba's "socialism" was the product of a revolution in 1959 that toppled one of the most corrupt U.S.-backed dictators of the day—Fulgencio Batista. The mass of Cubans were much better off liberated from the domination U.S. imperialism, with a government willing to commit social resources to, for example, a mass literacy campaign. The Cuban revolution inspired people throughout Latin America and around the world to struggle, whether against the domination of U.S. imperialism or their own homegrown elites.

So a Cuba under Castro was far better than a Cuba under Batista—or any new regime led by one of the U.S.-backed anti-communists who nursed dreams of overthrowing Castro.

But this isn't the same as socialism. Masses of Cubans were and are routinely mobilized in defense of the revolution, but they don't have a real say in how society is organized. That power remains in the hands of a small and generally unelected elite. On certain questions—for example, repressive measures against LGBT people—Cuba's rulers are guilty of violating basic democratic rights in ways that make a mockery of any claims to be socialist. But even if you believe that Cuba's elite desires to rule for the benefit of the people, the point is that they *rule*—as opposed to acting under a system that would hold them accountable to the democratic will of the majority.

The American socialist Hal Draper crystallized this discussion by talking about two fundamentally different "souls" of socialism. There is socialism from above—whether that means social democratic parties vying for office in capitalist democracies and trying to implement more liberal policies within the framework of the free market or a political elite that runs society in the name of socialism through bureaucratic control of the state. And there is socialism from below—a tradition that extends back to Marx and Engels, and puts the self-emancipation of the working class at its heart. Engels elaborated on the centrality of democracy and workers' power to socialism:

> It goes without saying that society cannot itself be free unless each individual is free. The old mode of production must therefore be revolutionized from top to bottom. Its place must be taken by an organization of production in which, on the one hand, no individual can put on to other persons his share of the productive labor ... and in which, on the other hand, productive labor, instead of being a means to the subjection of men, will become a means to their emancipation, by giving each individual the opportunity to develop and exercise all his faculties.

Fine words. So are there any examples of socialism existing in the world today? The answer is no. In fact, in the struggles of the past, we've only seen partial glimpses of what a future socialist society could look like. But those glimpses, along with the whole tradition of working-class struggle, show not only that socialism is possible, but also the outlines of how it can be organized to ensure democracy and freedom.

If you look at the biggest social upheavals of the last one hundred years—for example, the 1917 revolution in Russia and the few short years of an experiment in workers' power until the Stalinist counterrevolution; the revolutionary wave in Germany in the early 1920s; Spain's revolution in the 1930s; Portugal in the 1970s; to name a few—the centerpiece was mass participation. The heart of these struggles was the actions and experiences of the masses of people who took part in them.

One characteristic common to all of them is that at their

high points, before they were turned back, they created similar systems for the majority to make decisions about how to organize the struggle and the basic functioning of society. Each time, working-class democracy revolved around a structure of workers' councils. In Russia, for example, workers' councils (known by the Russian word *soviet*) developed spontaneously out of the 1905 revolution, and again in 1917. They first appeared as elected workplace committees, formed to organize around economic issues. But the need to respond to wider political questions led the councils to make links locally and then regionally.

It was natural for the soviets—created in the midst of struggle against the old order—to become the basis for workers to exercise their power in a new order. There was a direct connection between the councils' representation from workplaces and the need to decide how to use the wealth produced at those workplaces. And on this basis, it was possible for the soviets to reach out to other groups in society and offer them a voice.

John Reed, the American socialist and author of *Ten Days That Shook the World*, an eyewitness account of Russia in 1917, described the spirit of the soviets: "No political body more sensitive and responsive to the popular will was ever invented. And this was necessary, for in time of revolution, the popular will changes with great rapidity."

Russia's soviets and all of the examples of workers' councils in other countries over the years have shared similar features— immediate recall of anyone elected as a representative, so workers can control the people they vote for; not paying representatives more than the people they represent or allowing them to rise above anyone else's social level; elections taking place at mass meetings rather than in the isolation of the voting booth.

Many of the most basic features of such a system—meetings and discussions, democratic methods for making decisions—will be familiar to people who are activists today, or who have participated in a protest, building occupation, or a strike. As struggles and movements develop and mature, these building blocks of grassroots democracy can be tied together in bigger structures that reflect the will of larger numbers of people. The exact shape of such a system may change, but what's important is the democratic principle embodied in past struggles—the idea that representatives of the people have to be held *accountable* to the people.

Human Nature and Socialism

The heart of socialism is making equality a reality. Marx summed up this aim with a simple slogan: "From each according to their ability, to each according to their need." This idea often provokes a very strange objection: That human beings, given a chance to assure a livelihood for themselves, their families, their whole communities, and ultimately everyone in the whole world just won't have anything to do with it. Our human nature, we're told, will never tolerate a world of equality, even if it could be achieved. It's our natural impulse to compete, fight, envy, hate, and so on.

This alleged affliction isn't even left anymore to something insubstantial, like our "immortal souls," from which Christianity believes our flawed character originates. These days, barely a month seems to go by without some scientific authority announcing the discovery of the gene that determines violence or selfishness or criminality or some other form of behavior. Apparently, our instinct for wanting a bigger house than the next person is built into our cells. But is any of this true?

First of all, this view of human nature is hard to square with the acts of selflessness that are commonplace even under capitalism—parents' sacrifices for their children, family members' concern for their loved ones, people's commitment to their neighborhood or community. This spirit of solidarity can extend literally around the world in times of crisis. The destruction of New Orleans after Hurricane Katrina stirred offers of help from across the globe, including countries most in need of help themselves from the United States.

It's true that the spirit of giving doesn't spread through the whole of society. In particular, it seems to shrivel up and die the higher you get up the income ladder. Statistics from charitable organizations bear out the timeworn truth that people who can afford it least typically give the most of themselves. As a character in John Steinbeck's *The Grapes of Wrath* put it: "I'm learnin' one thing good … If you're in trouble or hurt or need—go to poor people. They're the only ones that'll help—the only ones."

The examples that we do see throughout society of competition, violence, and greed are better explained by economic and social circumstances, not some unchanging human nature. The reality of scarcity—that there isn't enough to go around—gives rise to the dog-eat-dog mentality.

Take the question of crime. First of all, many crimes that ought to be considered the most heinous—starting wars, forcing people to work in unsafe conditions, polluting the environment—aren't even against the law. But even if we limit ourselves to what most people understand to be "crimes," economic need looms largest among the reasons that people commit them. "The first great cause of crime is poverty," the great radical lawyer Clarence Darrow said in a speech to prisoners in 1914, "and we will never cure crime until we get rid of poverty."

If politicians really wanted to get "tough on crime," as they so often claim, they would take measures to eliminate the economic and social desperation that gives rise to crime, and promote policies that provide well-paying jobs, youth programs, child care, health care, and help for anyone in society who needs it. Instead, the perennial answer is more prisons and longer sentences—the "lock 'em up and throw away the key" answer. This attitude serves an ideological purpose—it deflects attention from the social causes of the problems in the world around us, and puts the focus on individual weakness or poor character or ill will. After all, if some kids are just prone to committing crimes, then what's the use of funding youth jobs programs to lift them out of poverty?

Socialists turn the blame around and focus on the social roots of crime. As the scientist Stephen Jay Gould wrote:

> Why imagine that specific genes for aggression or spite have any importance when we know that the brain's enormous flexibility permits us to be aggressive or peaceful, dominant or submissive, spiteful or generous? Violence, sexism and general nastiness are biological since they represent one subset of a possible range of behaviors. But peacefulness,

equality and kindness are just as biological—and we may see their influence increase if we can create social structures that permit them to flourish.

It follows that the struggle to create the circumstances for these positive behaviors to flourish is the key. Fundamentally, the socialist case is this: If the material circumstances that give rise to competition, greed, violence, and all the rest are eliminated, then we can imagine humanity acting permanently on the basis of the motivations we value: love, kindness, solidarity, hope.

Socialism would be about freeing people from the conditions that hold them down under capitalism, and giving them the opportunity to do what they really want to do—become doctors or scientists or artists or anything else they desire. We would use our technological knowledge to eliminate thankless and unfulfilling jobs, and share out equally the ones we couldn't. The goal would be to liberate all people to do the work they love—and to give them the leisure time to enjoy all the wonders of the world around them.

Capitalism stifles people's creativity. Only a minority is asked to put their minds to thinking about society—and most of them do it for the purpose of making themselves richer, not for achieving any common good. Imagine a society in which it mattered what ordinary people thought about what they were doing—where it mattered what an assembly-line worker thought about the pace of work, what a hospital worker thought about the availability of medical resources, what a student thought about how history is taught. That's a world in which people would become fully alive in a way they never will under capitalism.

CHAPTER FIVE

How Do We Change the System?

One event at the end of the first year of Barack Obama's presidency symbolized the gap between the promise of change that he had represented to so many people and the frustrating reality: a war president accepting the Nobel Peace Prize.

Obama owed his success in the election, at least during the Democratic primaries, to the perception that he was the main antiwar candidate. Yet there he was in Oslo, accepting the Nobel Peace Prize a week after announcing he would escalate the already-eight-year-old U.S. war on Afghanistan with a second troop surge.

Sure, Obama's Nobel speech started with the usual claims of "great humility" to be receiving such an honor—right before he delivered as ugly an example of American imperial arrogance as anything George W. Bush could have managed. "Whatever mistakes we have made," Obama pronounced, "the plain fact is this: the United States of America has helped underwrite global security for more than six decades with the blood of our citizens and the strength of our arms. The service and sacrifice of our men and women in uniform has promoted peace and prosperity from Germany to Korea."

Underwritten global security? Tell it to the relatives of the innocent Afghans torn to pieces by U.S. bombs dropped on wedding parties. Promoted peace and prosperity? Ask the people of East Timor after a quarter century of a U.S.-sanctioned genocide by Indonesia. Blood of *our* citizens? An Iraqi could tell you about the blood of *her* citizens, spilled to protect the U.S. government's control over Middle East oil.

If Obama's goal was to win the approval of right-wing Republicans—the ones accusing him of "palling around with terrorists" and pandering to crazies who think Obama was born in Kenya—he did succeed on that count. "I liked what he said," Sarah Palin chirped. Newt Gingrich praised "a very historic speech." Walter Russell Mead—whose title of Henry Kissinger senior fellow for U.S. foreign policy at the Council on Foreign Relations tells you everything you need to know about him—couldn't contain his delight:

> Barack Obama's acceptance speech for the Nobel Peace Prize was a carefully reasoned defense of a foreign policy that differs very little from George Bush's. He is winding down one war, escalating a second, and stepping up the pressure on Iran. He is asserting America's sovereign right to unilateral action in self-defense, while expressing the hope that this right will not need to be exercised.
>
> If Bush had said these things, the world would be filled with violent denunciations. When Obama says them, people purr. That is fine by me ... I've waxed lyrical about Obama's ability to sell our foreign policy to the world. He didn't just put lipstick on the pig; he gave it a makeover and sent it to charm school.

Obama's Nobel speech and the reaction of people like Mead was further evidence of a basic fact: Real change from the status quo will never come from electing a politician—especially not one who leads a political party dedicated to upholding that status quo.

People who want to see a different kind of society have to decide how to get there. The realistic alternative, we're told, is to work "through the system." In a country like the United States, the government is ultimately supposed to represent the "will of the people," so those who want to make a difference should follow the democratic process and "work from within." But the experience of the Obama administration tells a different story about whether the system can be changed from the inside.

Saying One Thing and Doing Another

Barack Obama's presidential campaign stirred more popular enthusiasm than anything to happen in mainstream politics for more than a generation. It was an invigorating mood after years of conservative domination in Washington. But the reality is that his administration has acted far more often like its hated predecessors.

In fact, for the Wall Street bailout, the Obama administration adopted almost exactly what the Bush administration came up with in its final months. Nothing about nationalization. No more than a toothless executive pay policy, with loopholes big enough for the fattest fat cat to slip through comfortably. Not even financial reforms and new regulations.

On health care, the administration declared a single-payer system—where the government covers everyone—"off the table" from the beginning. It then began negotiating with "stakeholders"—translation: the medical-insurance-pharmaceutical complex—and gradually bargained away even half-measures like the "public option" for the uninsured.

Even on issues where it would have been almost impossible to sink to the depths of the Bush administration, Obama has been a disappointment. On "national security" and civil liberties issues, the number of times the administration upheld policies from the Bush years—trial by military commissions, rendition of prisoners to allied regimes where torture is legal, warrantless wiretapping, use of executive powers to hinder the prosecution of U.S. officials for illegal acts—far outnumber the times it changed course.

Obama hasn't been a carbon copy of Bush. In June 2009, he marked LGBT Pride Month with a powerful statement decrying oppression and harassment that remained "all too common for members of the lesbian, gay, bisexual, and transgender (LGBT) community"—surely words that no one could imagine George W. Bush uttering. But within days of this declaration, the Obama Justice Department was in court defending both the Defense of Marriage Act and the military's "don't ask, don't tell" policy—two antigay measures Obama the candidate had promised to overturn—against legal challenges.

The list could go on and on. What it shows is that Barack Obama was never the crusader for change that he claimed to be on the campaign trail, but a much more conventional politician, as committed to the priorities of protecting the status quo as any other member of the two-party political establishment that runs Washington.

If you're wondering why the Wall Street bailout turned out the way it did, check the phone directory of senior staff at the Obama Treasury Department. You'll search in vain for figures associated with liberal policies—no one from the unions, no one from progressive think tanks, no community organizers. What you will find are plenty of former employees of super-bank Goldman Sachs.

Treasury Secretary Tim Geithner, while not a Goldman alumnus, is perfectly representative of the brand of people that make up the Obama administration—someone whose political views are bound up with the narrow world of the financial and political elite within which he has operated his entire professional life.

In the fall of 2009, the Associated Press used a Freedom of Information Act request to obtain Geithner's phone records and calendar while he was Treasury Secretary. What they showed, the AP reported, was that the CEOs of Goldman Sachs, Citigroup, and JPMorgan Chase were among a small core of "Wall Street executives who have known Geithner for years, whose multibillion-dollar companies survived the economic crisis with his help, and who can pick up the phone and reach the nation's most powerful economic official … Goldman, Citi and JPMorgan can get Geithner on the phone several times a day if necessary, giving them an unmatched opportunity to influence policy."

It would be hard to find a better example of how the Washington political system works. Ordinary people are supposed to be able to have an effect on government policy by voting for the candidates they support every two or four years. But if you run Goldman Sachs or Citigroup, you can have a far more direct effect on government policy every two or four *hours*, just by picking up the phone.

Many people who voted for Obama can see the effect that figures like Geithner have on administration policy. They don't always apply their criticisms to Obama himself—in part because they think he's being led astray from his correct instincts, the ones he expressed during the campaign, by bad advisers. But it makes much more sense, in light of the record, to recognize that Obama is part of the same corporate-money-soaked system he claimed that he wanted to change during the campaign.

Here, it helps to know that the Obama campaign's boast of having relied on "small donors" who gave $10, $20, and $50 is deceptive. According to the Campaign Finance Institute, Obama received 80 percent more contributions from large donors who gave $1,000 or more than from small donors who gave $200 or less. The number of small donors to the Obama campaign was still unprecedented. But so was the $210 million that the candidate raised from "bundlers" and large donors who gave $1,000 or more.

Another useful fact about Election 2008: The Democrats displaced the Republicans as the primary recipients of political donations from a number of important industries. As a New York University finance professor told the *Washington Post*, the threat of re-regulation on Wall Street meant that hedge funds "have a strong interest in becoming involved in the political process … In their analysis … Obama is likely to be successful, so it is very much in their advantage to have a strong voice with him." Seen in this light, the Obama administration's generous bailout terms for Wall Street and its reluctance to impose any costs on the bankers are easier to understand. The hedge funds did, in fact, buy "a strong voice" in the new administration.

The point isn't that Barack Obama is unique in being influenced by corporate power, but how much he has in common with business as usual in the Washington system. He isn't a reformer or maverick, but the leader of one of the two mainstream political parties that dominate American politics. Both parties have a long history, whatever their rhetoric to win votes, of running that system in the interests of the corporate and political elite, unless forced to act otherwise by pressure from below.

Of course, winning elections means getting ordinary people to vote for you, and no one would do that if the politicians were honest about how they really operate and who they really listen to. All candidates—even the most dyed-in-the-wool Republican tools of big business—talk about "serving the people" and giving ordinary Americans a better deal.

But this is a fraud—one that reflects the basic nature of government under capitalism. The politicians are the public face of a system that's set up to serve the rich. Their job is to say one thing to the majority of people to win their votes—while doing another for their real masters. For all his powerful speeches, Barack Obama isn't an exception but the rule.

Do the Democrats Make a Difference?

The two main parties of the American political system, the Republicans and Democrats, serve the status quo. Both parties are capitalist parties—in that they are devoted to protecting and maintaining capitalism and its institutions. But that doesn't mean they're exactly alike. The two parties have different roles to play—the Republicans relentlessly pursuing Corporate America's agenda, and the Democrats attempting to reconcile and co-opt opposition in order to preserve the essential interests of the establishment. On any given issue, most Republicans are likely to be more conservative than most Democrats. But the differences between the two parties are small when you compare them to the fundamental similarities that unite Republicans and Democrats.

Still, at election time, most people don't think about the similarities. Given a choice that's limited to the two parties, only the differences seem to matter. This is where the Democrats' undeserved reputation of being the "party of the people"—the party that's more likely to look out for the interests of labor and minorities—comes into play, no matter what their record in office has been.

A little history: First of all, the Democrats' image dates back only to the Great Depression of the 1930s. Initially, the "party of the people" was the party of the Southern slaveowners, with a smaller base in the North organized around corrupt political machines that ran big cities. That only changed because of President Franklin Delano Roosevelt's New Deal reforms, which laid the basis for many of the programs we associate with the federal government today—like Social Security and unemployment insurance.

These were important victories, and it's no wonder that working people look back on the politicians associated with them as friends of labor. But that's not how Roosevelt thought of himself. "[T]hose who have property [fail] to realize that I am the best friend the profit system ever had," Roosevelt said. Roosevelt carried out the New Deal reforms as a conscious effort to head off a social revolt caused by the Great Depression.

Roosevelt ran for president in 1932, with the country still in the grips of the crisis, but his platform didn't champion workers' rights or government jobs programs. On the contrary, he spent much of the campaign attacking his Republican opponent, the incumbent president Herbert Hoover, for "reckless" spending. Roosevelt promised to balance the budget by cutting government spending.

The scale of the economic crisis forced a different response once Roosevelt got in the White House. Nevertheless, the initiative for the first elements of the New Deal didn't come from idealistic social reformers but some of the country's leading businessmen, including General Electric's Gerard Swope and Walter Teagle of Standard Oil of New Jersey, who believed that state intervention was necessary to control the excesses of private capitalism.

Roosevelt and the "New Deal capitalists" recognized the need to make some concessions to popular demands. But their hand had to be forced at each step. Thus, the National Recovery Act's famous Clause 7(a), which protected the right of unions to bargain collectively with employers, was seen by some of its advocates as a means to promote employer-dominated "associations" of workers as an alternative to unions. It was only when workers themselves took up Clause 7(a) as a tool for organizing—often spontaneously, without prompting from conservative craft union leaders of the American Federation of Labor—that the new law took on real meaning. In other words, it took grassroots action to give pro-worker content to Roosevelt's reforms.

Roosevelt was under pressure from an explosion of struggle and protest—actions by the unemployed, the "Bonus March" of First World War veterans demanding promised benefits, the spread of direct action against evictions, and especially strikes and union organizing drives that culminated in the tidal wave of sit-down strikes in 1937. But every concession to popular demands was made grudgingly. The Social Security retirement program, for example, was a compromise measure. With its funding structure through a regressive payroll tax that determines the level of future benefits, it was specifically counterposed to a more radical social-welfare system that would have guaranteed a livable income for all seniors.

And there was a price to be paid for every gain—Roosevelt gave reforms in return for union votes. Initiatives for forming a political party to represent the labor movement were squashed, and Roosevelt succeeded in cementing the unions' misplaced loyalty to the Democrats that lasts to this day.

The Democrats played a similar role during the social upheavals of the 1960s. Presidents John F. Kennedy and Lyndon Johnson today have an entirely unearned reputation as antiracists

Grandad Norman got trapped!!! [handwritten margin note]

because they eventually supported some ci⸻
they had to be dragged into doing it.

Even though the votes of Blacks p⸻
House, Kennedy did his best to ignore t⸻
movement in the U.S. South. He and his⸻
eral Robert Kennedy, would meet priva⸻
movement, like Martin Luther King, Jr⸻
their influence to curb actions against the Southern power
structure and dampen expectations for change. It was only
after the Black struggle grew to explosive proportions that
Johnson pushed through the Civil Rights Act of 1964 and the
Voting Rights Act of 1965, the two key pieces of 1960s civil
rights legislation.

Figures like Roosevelt and Kennedy represent the best
face that the Democrats have to put forward to their liberal
base. But the party should have to answer for its ugly side,
too—bigots like West Virginia Senator Robert Byrd, a Klan
member in his long-ago younger years; or pro-war cheerleaders like Connecticut Senator Joe Lieberman (who isn't even a
Democrat anymore); or the long list of self-described "cen-
trists" who gravitated to the conservative Democratic Leadership Council (DLC) within the party.

The DLC's most famous former chair is Bill Clinton. At the
end of the Bush years in the late 2000s, there was a tendency
for many people to look back on Clinton's presidency with rose-
colored glasses. They forgot the real record of the most conservative Democrat to inhabit the White House since before
Roosevelt—a trail of broken promises that should serve as an

son in how Democrats will say one thing to win votes
another in office. When Clinton outmaneuvered the Re-
blicans to win reelection comfortably in 1996, one disgrun-
tled conservative snarled: "The good news is that we're going
to have a Republican president in 1996. The bad news is that it
will be Bill Clinton."

The problem with the Democrats isn't the individuals—as
infuriating as some are. The problem is the institution that
bends the individuals to its purposes.

Peter Camejo, the veteran socialist who was independent
presidential candidate Ralph Nader's running mate in 2004,
used to point to the Democratic presidential candidate that
year, John Kerry, and remind audiences that Kerry was among
the Vietnam veterans who testified against the war before Congress in the 1970s. Kerry wasn't the most radical, but he did
coin a phrase that crystallized the feelings of the growing antiwar majority: "How do you ask a man to be the last man to die
for a mistake?" Compare that to Kerry's wishy-washy attitude
to the Bush administration invasion of Iraq—highlighted by his
campaign trail comment that he had voted for funding the war
before he voted against it.

So what happened to John Kerry? Camejo would ask. Simple: That's what thirty years inside the Democratic Party
machine—committed to compromise and upholding the interests of the American business and political establishment—
does to someone.

The point applies not just to Democratic officeholders, but
the liberal organizations whose view of politics is limited to the

horizons of the Democratic Party. Groups like the National Organization for Women see their job as speaking for a section of the party's liberal base. But they have adapted themselves to serve their relationship to the Democrats—which means accepting compromises in order to assure that the greater evil, the Republicans, doesn't triumph over the lesser evil, the Democrats.

This logic of "lesser evilism" is incredibly corrosive. Consider the example of "welfare reform"—proposed in the 1990s by the Republicans as a justification for dismantling programs that provided aid to some of the most vulnerable and desperately poor people in society. Four years into his presidency, Bill Clinton took up the Republicans' proposal and signed it into law.

Welfare "reform" was an especially mean-spirited piece of legislation whose victims were people who were least able to speak up for themselves. But the liberal groups that could have organized a response insisted it was more important to stand behind Clinton in the 1996 election, for fear of getting something worse—a Republican victory. "This is a bad bill, but a good strategy," said New York representative Gary Ackerman, explaining why he was voting for a welfare bill that he opposed. "In order to continue economic and social progress, we must keep President Clinton in office ... Sometimes, in order to make progress and move ahead, you have to stand up and do the wrong thing."

"Stand up and do the wrong thing." This is what it means to accept "lesser evilism"—the idea that people who believe in ideals of justice and peace should hold their nose and vote for

Democrats who believe in neither justice nor peace because they're the lesser evil.

It's certainly understandable why people disgusted by the Republicans and their ugly rhetoric would want to stop the right wing at any cost. It seems like common sense that you should support the Democrats, not because you think they'll accomplish anything, but in the hope that you can stop something worse from happening. But in reality, this is exactly the wrong way to stop the "worst" from happening. The people who voted for Bill Clinton because they hated the Republicans' cruel, victim-blaming proposals got those same measures served up by a Democratic president. The people who voted for Barack Obama because they'd had enough of George Bush's war on the world got the same war policies presented more articulately.

The next time someone demands that you renounce the idea that Obama's Democrats are no different from Sarah Palin's Republicans, remember this: They are different, of course—but the distance between where Democrats and Republicans stand today is not nearly so large as the distance that the two parties *together* have shifted to the right over the course of the last thirty years.

If Barack Obama and Bill Clinton look better compared to George W. Bush and Ronald Reagan, it shouldn't be forgotten that these latter-day Democrats are plainly *more* conservative than plenty of presidents who came before them—Republicans included. Thus, Republican president Richard Nixon launched more antidiscrimination and affirmative action programs than

Bill Clinton. That's not because Nixon was more liberal. On the contrary, he was a miserable right-winger. But Nixon was under pressure to act from the mass social movements of the 1960s and early 1970s, something that neither Clinton nor Obama have faced.

As the historian Howard Zinn put it in an interview with *Socialist Worker* right after George W. Bush took office in 2001, "There's hardly anything more important that people can learn than the fact that the really critical thing isn't who is sitting in the White House, but who is *sitting in*—in the streets, in the cafeterias, in the halls of government, in the factories. Who is protesting, who is occupying offices and demonstrating—those are the things that determine what happens."

Can the System Be Fixed?

On the whole, politicians have a pretty pathetic reputation, no matter what party they're in. In the opinion surveys asking people who they trust more, politicians regularly battle used car dealers for the cellar of the league. But most people have more respect for the institutions of the U.S. political system—or at least the founding ideals and traditions of that system. In fact, some people with a radical critique of what's wrong with society put their hopes in a struggle to sweep out the corrupt egomaniacs in charge today and reclaim those traditions for the people.

Getting rid of crooks and con artists is always a good thing. But the problems with the "world's greatest democracy" go beyond the individuals who scrambled to the top of the heap. The system itself is rigged in all sorts of ways to be the opposite of a "government of the people, by the people, for the people."

How is it rigged? For one thing, after the experience of the 2000 presidential election, it's hard to say that voting has anything to do with who holds power in Washington. George W. Bush lost the popular vote in 2000 by half a million votes. But he won the White House anyway in the Electoral College, a relic of the eighteenth century designed to limit democracy and protect the interests of slaveowners. And that was only possible because a 5–4 majority of the unelected justices of the U.S. Supreme Court decided that the state of Florida didn't need to count every ballot cast in the election—only the ones that gave a victory to the candidate whose father or his cronies had appointed them.

The fraud in Florida exposed some of the dirty secrets of American democracy—like the extent to which the right to vote is denied outright. To begin with, 5.3 million people, or one in every thirty-nine adults, have lost their voting rights, some permanently, as a result of felony convictions. Other people are disenfranchised because they were born outside the United States. According to the census in 2000, there were between 30 million and 40 million foreign-born people in the United States—more than 20 million of them legal residents but non-citizens, who are denied the right to vote in all but a handful of localities.

And this is just to look at the formal restrictions on "democracy." The way voting and elections take place in the United States—from the often-convoluted rules for registering to the perennial screwups on Election Day itself, not to mention the mind-numbing campaigning we're made to endure for months beforehand—seems almost designed to discourage even people who are qualified to vote from getting to the polls. In 2008, the presidential election produced the highest voter turnout in forty years, a sign of the enthusiasm generated by the Obama campaign. But the total turnout rate was still only 56.8 percent of the voting age population—meaning more than two of every five people who could have cast a ballot, or should have been eligible to, didn't.

When you strip away the myths, elections in the United States look more like an empty ritual—one that perpetuates a common political power structure, rather than offers a choice between real alternatives. In elections for the House of Representatives between 1982 and 2004, incumbent lawmakers won reelection more than 95 percent of the time—pretty much the same rate as the sham elections at the height of the Stalinist dictatorship in the ex-USSR.

At the beginning of the twentieth century, President Woodrow Wilson gave a more accurate description of what happens in the U.S. political system:

> Suppose you go to Washington and try to get at your government. You will always find that while you are politely listened to, the men really consulted are the men who have the big stake—the big bankers, the big manufacturers and the big masters of commerce ... The masters of the government of the United States are the combined capitalists and manufacturers of the United States.

A century later, these words ring more true than ever. There's nothing subtle about the way Corporate America buys influence in Washington. The health care industry spent untold sums making sure reform measures that might threaten their profits were pushed "off the table"—and the legislation that did emerge was shaped to their interests.

Plenty of money goes to the campaigns of important legislators—like Max Baucus, the Democratic senator who put together the Senate's health care "reform" bill. But in some ways, campaign contributions are a sideshow to the real supermarket for the buying and selling of influence in Washington—corporate lobbying. The major health care industry groups spent an average of $1.4 million *every day* to lobby in 2009, for a total of more than $500 million, according to election watchdog group Common Cause.

The Washington system oozes money. But it's not like the men and women with seats in Congress are strangers to it before they got to the capital. The Center for Responsive Politics analysis of annual financial disclosures made by members of the House and Senate estimated that nearly half were millionaires in 2009—a total of 237 lawmakers out of 535. The median net worth for senators was $1.8 million, and $622,254 for representatives.

There's a reason why so many members of Congress are rich. It helps with the high cost of getting elected if you have your own personal fortune. Two decades ago, the average cost of a winning campaign for the House of Representatives was already over $400,000. By 2008, it had more than tripled to $1.4 million. The average cost of a *losing* House race in 2008 was nearly half a million dollars, almost $100,000 more than it cost to win twenty years before.

So the elected representatives in Washington aren't exactly representative of ordinary people. Even without corporate campaign contributions and intensive lobbying, members of Congress are inclined toward the same world view as the heads of banks and corporations because so many belong to the same class.

These are some of the reasons why socialists don't put our hopes in electing the right politicians into office. Even when there are genuinely independent, left-wing candidates to support and vote for in elections—such as Ralph Nader's independent presidential campaigns—voting isn't the most important way to be politically active.

The government is supposed to be a neutral force in society—one that can make fair and even-handed laws that treat everyone equally. But governments in capitalist societies aren't even-handed at all. They ultimately act in the interests of the ruling class.

One reason is because, as we've seen, the corporate elite dominates the system of legalized bribery that funds the mainstream parties. But there's more to the question. Governments consist of more than elected representatives. There are the unelected bureaucracies that make crucial decisions affecting people's lives. There's the judicial side of the U.S. government—federal judges all the way up to the Supreme Court who never face an election. And standing behind all this is what Frederick Engels called "bodies of armed men"—the police and the army. Formally, the Pentagon may be answerable to elected politicians, but in reality, it's a power unto itself.

Because of this, even people with every intention of "making a difference" when they try to get themselves elected find that, once in office, rather than being able to pull the levers of power to change the system, the levers of power pull them. At best, they end up managing the system they expected to change.

Let's indulge in a daydream. Let's imagine that Barack Obama arrived in the White House ready to fight for the policies supported by a majority of the people who voted for him. We'll pretend that Obama intended to hold the bankers' feet to the fire with tough new regulations and pay restrictions, to champion a strong government role in the health care system, to curb the abuses of private industry, and to get *all* U.S. troops out of Iraq as soon as possible.

What would happen? Within minutes of taking office, this alternative version of Obama would have gotten a visit from his Treasury Secretary and the chair of the government's central bank, the Federal Reserve. They would tell him that Wall Street and Corporate America wanted nothing to do with his agenda unless he compromised, and would take action if he persisted—for example, sending their money out of the country so it couldn't be taxed, and causing turbulence on the financial markets. As for the Pentagon, the chair of the Joint Chiefs of Staff would deliver a similar message—no cooperation unless the White House "moderated" its position.

Even the president of the United States—the most powerful man in the world—can't personally dictate political changes if they threaten the interests of the ruling elite in any serious way. Banks, corporations, the Pentagon, the political establishment—

together they have too many weapons at their command, inside and outside the government, for even the most determined politician to overcome by themselves.

And remember: This fantasy version of Obama isn't even very radical. If I or any of my socialist friends were somehow magically placed in the Oval Office instead of Obama—or any other political office, for that matter—we'd face even more ruling-class resistance. The problem is that without a more fundamental change in what government represents and how decisions get made, even a socialist president would be limited in what she or he could do.

These are the odds that face someone trying to accomplish something substantial by working within the system. The political system in the United States—or any country, for that matter—isn't a neutral vehicle that can be redirected toward meeting our goals. The deck is stacked against anyone who tries to pose a serious challenge to the interests and priorities of the ruling class from within an institution designed to protect its rule.

And think about the effects on the people who try to work from the inside. However good their intentions and strong their commitment, the "realistic" response when faced with resistance is to bargain and make concessions—to try to find some arrangement that's acceptable to all sides. But when this becomes the priority, politics turns into the art of compromise rather than a campaign to accomplish something. And that shapes the plans and the outlook of the people trying to make change from inside a rigged system.

So elected representatives are only one part of government under capitalism. And in a number of tragic examples in history, they've turned out to be the dispensable part—when sections of the ruling class decided to ditch democracy and rule by force. The most infamous case of this comes from Chile. The socialist Salvador Allende was elected president in 1970 on a mild program of reform that included nationalizing parts of the economy. Many people took this as a sign that socialism could be elected into power. But for the next three years, Chile's bosses—and their international partners, especially in the United States—did everything they could to sabotage Allende. U.S. secretary of state Henry Kissinger declared: "I don't see why we need to stand by and watch a country go communist because of the irresponsibility of its own people." Allende compromised, but it wasn't enough. When the time was ripe, Chile's generals made their move, launching a coup that claimed the lives of tens of thousands of Chilean workers, along with Allende's.

Our rulers prefer to dominate a political system that provides the appearance of democracy, but which gives them most of the influence over what decisions get made and how. But if any force arises to threaten this rule, they're willing to dispense with democracy and rule by brute force.

Taken together, these facts about the political system under capitalism show why socialists conclude that the system can't be reformed—why capitalist society can't be changed fundamentally by working through political structures designed to defend the status quo.

Instead of trying to get well-intentioned politicians elected to make what changes they can, our goal is far bigger—a social struggle to overturn and remake the whole system. That is what a revolution is about—taking away the power of the people at the top of society to make unaccountable decisions that affect our lives, getting rid of a state machine organized to preserve the system as it exists today, and building a completely different and more democratic system to make decisions about society.

This doesn't mean socialists don't care about reforms. We spend most of our time as part of efforts to win changes in the existing system. These reforms make workers' lives easier and increase their power in the here and now. And they make people more confident in the struggle to win further change. As the revolutionary Rosa Luxemburg wrote:

> Can we counterpose the social revolution, the transformation of the existing social order, our final goal, to social reforms? Certainly not. The daily struggle for reforms, for the amelioration of the condition of the workers within the framework of the existing social order, and for democratic institutions, offers to [socialists] the only means of engaging in the proletarian class war and working in the direction of the final goal—the conquest of political power and the suppression of wage labor. Between social reforms and revolution there exists … an indissoluble tie. The struggle for reforms is its means; the social revolution, its aim.

Socialists fight for reforms. But reforms by themselves aren't enough—because they can be taken back if the movement retreats. We need a revolution because capitalist society can't be fundamentally and permanently changed in any other way.

CHAPTER SIX

"If There Is No Struggle, There Is No Progress"

When socialists talk about the need for a revolution to transform society, we're accused of being unrealistic and utopian. Do we really expect a revolution to ever take place in the United States?

Actually, the question isn't *whether* a revolution can take place in the United States. The question is whether *another* revolution can take place. The United States has already had two revolutions. The first, in 1776, overthrew colonial rule by Britain's monarchy and produced a new nation, organized around a representative government and probably the widest system of democracy known to the world to that point. But there were gaping holes—the crime of slavery was left untouched, and only a minority of men qualified to vote as property-holders.

As a result of the contradictions left over from the first revolution, the United States experienced another social revolution ninety years later—the Civil War of 1861–65, which destroyed the Southern system of slavery. Today, credit for "freeing the slaves" usually goes to Abraham Lincoln and perhaps a few army generals. But the North would never have won the war against slavery without the active participation of masses of people. Black slaves themselves played a crucial role, as did the agitators of the abolitionist movement in the North. Also central to the transformation were the soldiers of the Northern army—many of whom started fighting without a clear idea of the war's aim, but were convinced over time of the need to abolish slavery.

These weren't socialist revolutions. The War of 1776 and the Civil War were revolutions against colonial rule and against slavery, which left the economic setup of capitalism intact. But no one would dispute that these struggles transformed U.S. society. And they certainly disprove the picture of a country that has always been stable and politically moderate.

The years since have produced other uprisings that can't be called revolutions, but that certainly shook the United States to its foundations—the struggle for the eight-hour day during the 1880s; the "great red year" of 1919, when one in five U.S. workers was on strike; the 1930s battles for labor's rights; and the 1960s, an era that opened with the civil rights movement in the South and closed with struggles that questioned almost everything about U.S. society, from the U.S. war in Vietnam to the oppression of women and gays and lesbians.

Looking at the past this way—at its social conflicts and political struggles—is different from what passes for history in school. To begin with, the way history is usually taught—remembering the names of famous people and the dates when they did something important—is upside down. The course of history depends most of all not on what a few "great men" did or thought, but on the actions of huge numbers of people, especially during the times when they organize themselves in rebellions and revolutions. It's not that figures like Thomas Jefferson and Abraham Lincoln are unimportant. But what they did and what they're remembered for today were shaped by the actions of masses of people who aren't remembered at all. As Lincoln himself wrote in a letter, "I claim not to have controlled events, but confess plainly that events have controlled me."

The socialist Bertolt Brecht crystallized the point in a poem called "Questions from a Worker Who Reads":

Who built Thebes of the seven gates?
In the books you will find the names of kings.
Did the kings haul up the lumps of rock?
And Babylon, many times demolished
Who raised it up so many times? In what houses
Of gold-glittering Lima did the builders live?
Where, the evening that the Wall of China was finished
Did the masons go? ...

The young Alexander conquered India.
Was he alone?
Caesar beat the Gauls.
Did he not have even a cook with him?
Philip of Spain wept when his armada
Went down. Was he the only one to weep?
Frederick the Second won the Seven Years' War. Who
Else won it?

Every page a victory.
Who cooked the feast for the victors?
Every ten years a great man.
Who paid the bill?

Something else flows from a socialist view of history. We're taught that political and social change, if it happens at all, takes place at a safe, gradual pace. Let any group of people organize to show their opposition to an injustice, and they're certain to be told to be patient—to let the system work.

But this goes against the whole history of the struggle for justice and equality. So, for example, in the first half of the nineteenth century, virtually every U.S. politician, in the North and South, believed that the enslavement of Blacks would die out eventually if the Southern slave system was left alone. They were wrong; the slaveocracy grew more powerful all the time because of the importance of cotton production to the world economy. It took the Civil War to put an end to this horror.

Name a movement in U.S. history: civil rights, women's right to vote, the eight-hour day, opposition to U.S. wars abroad—each one was faced with calls to slow down and be moderate. "For years now," Martin Luther King, Jr. wrote in his "Letter from a Birmingham Jail," "I have heard the word 'Wait!' It rings in the ear of every Negro with piercing familiarity. This 'Wait' has almost always meant 'Never.' We must come to see, with one of our distinguished jurists, that 'justice too long delayed is justice denied.'" The determination of activists not to "wait" is why the civil rights movement ended in victory.

The United States is supposed to be the most stable of countries. But revolutions and social upheavals are a constant theme, and they leave a political legacy behind, even when they recede or retreat. Most of the reforms that workers take for granted today are a product of those upheavals. Unemployment insurance, for example, was introduced as part of President Franklin Roosevelt's New Deal program of the 1930s. Roosevelt didn't come up with the idea, and he certainly didn't embrace it from the beginning. He was forced to adopt it by the crisis of the Great Depression and the threat of mass social pressure. Roosevelt ends up with the credit in the history books. But this doesn't change the fact that he was *forced* to act.

Struggle is the key. The great abolitionist leader Frederick Douglass made this plain with these words:

> The whole history of the progress of human liberty shows that all concessions yet made to her august claims have been born of earnest struggle … If there is no struggle, there is no progress. Those who profess to favor freedom and yet deprecate agitation are men who want crops without plowing up the ground, they want rain without thunder and lightning. They want the ocean without the awful roar of its mighty waters. The struggle may be a moral one, or it may be a physical one, and it may be both moral and physical, but it must be a struggle. Power concedes nothing without a demand. It never did, and it never will.

A Power Greater than Their Hoarded Gold

For hundreds if not thousands of years, most societies around the world have been divided between exploiters and exploited—between a ruling class of people that runs society in its own interest and much larger exploited classes whose labor is the source of their rulers' wealth and power. Under each system, the biggest conflicts have been between these classes—over who rules, who gets ruled over, and how. As Karl Marx and Frederick Engels put it in *The Communist Manifesto:*

"The history of all hitherto existing society is the history of class struggles. Freeman and slave, patrician and plebeian, lord and serf, guildmaster and journeyman, in a word, oppressor and oppressed, stood in constant opposition to one another, carried on an uninterrupted, now hidden, now open fight ..."

In all these societies, the oppressed have dreamed of a world of equality and justice where their oppression would end. And they have struggled for it—from the slave rebellion against the Roman Empire led by Spartacus to the peasant uprisings in Europe, among others.

So the ideals of socialism aren't new. But achieving them has only been a possibility for the last few centuries—in most parts of the world, for just the last hundred years. Why? Because socialism can't be organized on the basis of scarcity. Unless there's enough to go around, there's certain to be a scramble over who gets what, and that scramble is bound to produce a class society, in which one group of people organizes the system to make sure they do get enough, even if others go without. Whatever their advances over the past, societies before capitalism were unable to produce enough to end scarcity for good. Only under capitalism has human knowledge and technology been raised to the point where it would be possible to feed every person on the planet, clothe them, put a roof over their heads, and so on.

Under capitalism, there's no longer any natural reason for poverty to exist. But abolishing poverty means getting rid of a system that causes it—and that requires a social force capable of defeating it. Marx and Engels argued that in the process of its development, capitalism produced "its own gravediggers"—

the working class, with the power to overturn the system and establish a new society not divided between rulers and ruled.

Why did Marx and Engels talk about the working class? Not because workers suffer the most under capitalism. Socialists focus on the position that workers occupy in the capitalist economy. Their labor produces the profits that make the system run, so the working class as a whole, besides being the vast majority in society, has a special power that no other social group has to paralyze the system—to bring the profit system to a halt by not working.

French workers have shown this power repeatedly in recent decades. In 2006, for example, students began the fight against a new labor law proposed by a right-wing government that would have created a two-year trial period for any newly hired worker under age twenty-six, during which they could be fired without notice. When the country's main union federations called several one-day general strikes, France ground to a halt, with schools, public transportation, government offices, and a range of industries and services shut down. After one strike day in April brought three million people into the streets for protests across the country, the government backed down and withdrew the law.

Struggles that aren't immediately about labor issues can have a deeper impact if they involve workers exercising their power *as* workers. That was the case in apartheid South Africa, for example—where the rise of the Black workers' struggles in the 1980s shook the system more dramatically than all the battles that came before, ushering in the final days of the racist regime.

A *general* strike by workers throughout the economy can paralyze a whole country and bring a government to its knees. This happened in Poland in 1980 with the revolt of the Solidarnosc trade union. The upheaval began with a strike by shipyard workers in Gdansk, but soon spread to involve ten million workers across the country. Within weeks, democratically organized workers' committees sprang up to organize the strike and make decisions about how to provide essential services. The so-called socialist government—in reality, a repressive dictatorship—was powerless to restore order for more than a year. Before the strike, Polish workers would never have guessed that they could rock a seemingly all-powerful police state. But they cut off the lifeblood of the system—the wealth that they created with their labor.

Struggles organized on the basis of class have the potential of uniting the working majority throughout society, so all the have-nots fight on a common basis—not only for the demands they have in common, but for the special demands of oppressed groups. But workers only have this power if they're united. "Labor in white skin cannot emancipate itself where it is branded in Black skin," Marx wrote about slavery in the United States.

One of the most common criticisms of Marxism is that it focuses on a class that has been shrinking in importance and numbers as capitalism has aged. What the people who say this really mean is that in advanced countries, the blue-collar industrial working class has been decreasing as a proportion of the workforce as a whole. Internationally, the size of the industrial working class is bigger than ever—and even in advanced countries, it remains an important part of the economy.

More importantly, though, the idea that Marxists only care about industrial workers is a stereotype—one that goes along with a picture of the "proletariat" (to use Marx's term for the working class) as all male, working only in factories, and engaged in manual labor. Actually, Marx defined the working class not by the kind of work people did, but by their position in society—as "a class of laborers who live only so long as they find work, and who find work only so long as their labor increases capital," he wrote. In other words, the working class consists of people who have to sell their ability to work for a wage in order to survive. This applies not only to blue-collar factory workers, but to people who work in offices, the service sector, and so on.

So when Marxists talk about the working class, we don't mean the minority of people who fit into the narrow blue-collar occupation category. We mean the vast majority of people in society—in a country like the United States, something like 75 percent of the population.

Changes in the U.S. labor movement give a sense of the diversity of the modern working class. According to the Center for Economic and Policy Research, in 2008, women made up more than 45 percent of unionized workers, up from 35 percent a quarter century before. Latinos were the fastest growing ethnic group, having doubled their representation in unions in twenty-five years—and only one in ten unionized workers had a manufacturing job.

Nearly every country in the world today has a big working class, and the struggles of recent decades have shown the emergence of the working class as a powerful social force in poor countries. It's impossible, for example, to talk about Chávez's Venezuela without recognizing the role of the working-class movement in fighting for workers' control in factories—or the insurrectionary uprisings in Bolivia that set the stage for Evo Morales's election victories. In China, the regime's neoliberal strategy for letting the free market rip has been accompanied by a huge wave of strikes—in 2008, there were 127,000 "mass incidents," the government's deliberately vague term for strikes, protests, and riots.

When Marx and Engels were writing in the middle of the nineteenth century, the international working class was tiny—perhaps two or three million people, concentrated in Britain, a few countries in northwestern Europe, and along the north-eastern coast of the United States. Today, there are more workers in South Korea alone than there were around the world in Marx and Engels's time.

Everywhere across the globe, people's lives are shaped by the fact that they have to work to survive. But the flip side of this reality is that workers have enormous power. The final words of Marx and Engels's *Communist Manifesto* are more relevant today than ever: "The proletarians have nothing to lose but their chains. They have a world to win."

Can Workers Change Society?

If we were to judge only from what we see around us every day, it might be hard to have confidence that the majority of people can organize themselves to achieve a socialist society.

Most working people aren't revolutionaries. A significant number of them voted for John McCain, Sarah Palin, and the Republicans in the 2008 election. And even those who oppose the pro-corporate, pro-war agenda of the Washington establishment accept a number of ideas that justify the status quo most of the time—the old cliché that you can't fight City Hall, the belief that people at the top of society are somehow specially qualified to run it, and on and on.

This is partly because we're continually exposed to various institutions that are in the business of reinforcing these myths and prejudices. The mass media are one example. Watch cable TV news, and you'll see sensationalized stories about crime and violence or titillating celebrity gossip—while discussions about the real issues that affect people's lives get shortchanged. The poor are stereotyped and scapegoated, while the wealth and power of the rich are celebrated. Even shows meant as entertainment tend to reinforce the conventional wisdom.

Or take the education system, which is plainly designed to encourage conformity. Except for the minority of students being trained to rule society, the experience of school is usually alienating. Students are taught to compete against each other from Kindergarten and even before. The underlying objective is to encourage students to accept the conditions they see around them rather than challenge them.

With all the selfish and mean-spirited ideas actively promoted by these institutions of authority, it's a wonder that any sense of solidarity survives under capitalism. Yet it obviously does. This is most obvious in the outpourings of charity in cases of social disasters, like a famine or an earthquake. But even on a day-to-day basis, society simply couldn't function without a basic sense of cooperation and sacrifice among ordinary people—within families, for example, or among coworkers.

The point is that capitalist society obscures this basic decency—because the system is organized around greed and self-interest. Obviously, those in charge get ahead by being as greedy as possible. But working people are forced, whether they like it or not, to participate in a rat race that they have no control over. They're pitted against one another and required to compete just to keep their job or maintain their standard of living—a struggle every day that usually feels like it takes over our lives.

As a result, the idea of people uniting for social change can seem distant and unrealistic at times. Powerlessness produces what appears to be apathy among people—about their own future and the future of society.

This is why it isn't enough for socialists to talk about why socialism will make an excellent alternative to capitalism. It's also necessary to talk about the struggle to get there, because that struggle transforms people and gives them confidence in their own power. As Karl Marx put it, "Revolution is necessary not only because the ruling class cannot be overthrown in any other way, but also because the class overthrowing it can only in a revolution succeed in ridding itself of all the muck of ages and become fit to found society anew."

The act of fighting back is the first step in challenging the prejudices learned from living in the capitalist rat race. This can be seen in even a small strike. Strikes almost always start over a specific workplace issue—demands around wages and benefits, for example. But whatever the original grievance, striking workers who may have thought of themselves as law-abiding citizens are acting in a way that goes against what society teaches them. Fighting back also requires unity. So striking workers are often forced to question the divisions built up in their ranks—between Black and white, between men and women, between native born and immigrant. As the strike goes on, feelings of solidarity and a sense of the wider issues at stake start to become as important as the original issues.

The changes that take place can be profound. In December 2008, when workers at Republic Windows & Doors in Chicago learned that their factory was closing down and they wouldn't even get the severance package guaranteed them in their contract, they decided they wouldn't stand for it—literally. The Republic workers sat in—one of the first factory occupations in the United States since the sit-down strikes of the 1930s.

The Republic occupation galvanized the local labor movement. Groups of workers from unions across the city came day after day to lend their support and listen to speakers at rallies. Activists from the immigrant rights movement that had turned out hundreds of thousands of people for the May Day mega-marches in previous years reconnected and exchanged ideas with new allies. So did activists from other movements—after two hundred demonstrators rallied outside the Cook County Building as part of a day of action for same-sex marriage, many of them marched the several blocks to a protest outside the Bank of

America building to demand justice for the Republic workers. Weeks later, after the occupation had ended in victory, the Republic workers sent a representative to a meeting on the future of the LGBT struggle—to emphasize how the workers had come to see their own fight for justice as linked to other struggles in society.

In the course of any struggle, activists committed to the fight around a particular issue have to grapple with similar issues: What kind of change do we want? Who are our allies? How are we connected to other struggles? How do we organize to achieve what we want?

Take the example of the abolitionists fighting slavery in the nineteenth century—the movement that gave us Frederick Douglass's famous words: "If there is no struggle, there is no progress." That was actually a hard-earned conclusion for abolitionists operating in a world where the prevailing wisdom was that slavery would wither away and American society's better nature would prevail. There was a broad range of people committed to the cause, but with different ideas and strategies. Ultimately, the movement couldn't go forward until abolitionists had reached the conclusion that slavery would *not* wither away—that the slave power was built into the economy, the government, the press, and every social institution, and that the people who wanted to abolish it would have to organize themselves and take action.

Likewise, think of the Black college students who joined the civil rights movement. The prevailing hope at first was that civil disobedience would embarrass the federal government into acting against segregation. In 1960, one member of the newly formed Student Nonviolent Coordinating Committee could tell a reporter that she was motivated by traditional American values. If only Blacks were given educational opportunities, she said, "maybe someday, a Negro will invent one of our [nuclear] missiles."

A few years later, many SNCC members considered themselves revolutionaries. They had been through the Freedom Rides to desegregate interstate bus lines, the murder of civil rights workers during the Freedom Summer voter registration project in 1964, and the Democratic Party's betrayal of civil rights delegates at its 1964 national convention. These experiences convinced them that the struggle against racial injustice could only be won by linking it to the fight against other injustices—and for a different kind of society altogether.

This transformation was repeated throughout the 1960s and early 1970s. White college students who volunteered for Freedom Summer used the skills they learned from the civil rights movement to organize the struggle against the U.S. war in Vietnam. The Black Power movement in the North gave opponents of the war a clearer view of other injustices that needed to be fought. Activists from the antiwar movement in turn launched the struggle for women's rights, including the right to choose abortion. Out of all these struggles, the revolutionary left was reborn—in the United States and around the world—during the 1960s.

The struggles of the 1960s are proof that ideas can change with enormous speed. In periods of social upheaval, millions upon millions of people who had devoted their energy to all sorts of other things suddenly turn their attention to the question of transforming society.

The biggest struggles of all—revolutions that overturn the existing social order—produce the most extraordinary changes in people. What's most striking about the history of revolutions is the way that ordinary people, trained all their lives to be docile and obedient, suddenly find their voice.

The caricature of revolution passed off by many historians is of a small group of armed fanatics seizing control of the government and running it to enrich themselves. In the first instance, this obscures the main source of violence in society—the violence committed every single day in a multitude of ways in a society based on oppression and injustice. The great writer Mark Twain gave the lie to all the pious lectures about violence in revolutions when he defended the French Revolution of 1789, with its principles of liberty, equality, and brotherhood, against those who dismissed it as a "reign of terror" incited by blood-crazed mobs:

> There were two Reigns of Terror, if we would but remember it and consider it: the one wrought murder in hot passion, the other in heartless cold blood; the one lasted mere months, the other lasted a thousand years; the one inflicted death on ten thousand persons, the other upon a hundred millions … A city cemetery could contain the coffins filled by that brief Terror, which we have all been so diligently taught to shiver at and mourn over, but all France could hardly contain the coffins filled by that older and real Terror, which none of us has been taught to see in its vastness or pity as it deserves.

In addition to the hypocrisy about violence and revolution, there is another misconception—that socialism is something achieved by a small conspiratorial group. Such groups have organized revolutions. But a *socialist* revolution can't be carried out by a minority—even a minority that genuinely wants to improve the lives of the majority. That's because the heart of socialism is mass participation. As the Russian revolutionary Leon Trotsky put it:

> The most indubitable feature of a revolution is the direct interference of the masses in historic events. In ordinary times, the state—be it monarchical or democratic—elevates itself above the nation, and history is made by specialists in that line of business—kings, ministers, bureaucrats, parliamentarians, journalists. But at those crucial moments when the old order becomes no longer endurable to the masses, they break over the barriers excluding them from the political arena, sweep aside their traditional representatives, and create by their own interference the initial groundwork for a new regime ... The history of a revolution is for us, first of all, a history of the forcible entrance of the masses into the realm of rulership over their own destiny.

The right-wing writers who pass judgment on revolutions tend to focus on the endpoint—the armed insurrection to topple a government and seize political control. But this is only the final act of a revolution. It's the climax of a much longer period of struggle in which the rulers of society face a growing crisis, at the same time as workers become more confident of their own power.

At the beginning of the process, the goals for change can be modest—a few reforms in the way the system operates. But the struggle to change this or that aspect of society raises deeper questions. People begin to see the connections between the struggles that they're involved in and other issues—and the nature of the system itself. Organizing these struggles gives workers a further sense of their ability to run society for themselves. The act of taking over political power is the final step of a revolution that has already been felt in every workplace, in every neighborhood, and in every corner of society.

Ten Days that Shook the World

The Russian Revolution of 1917 is the only socialist revolution so far to succeed and survive for any length of time. Though the experience of workers' power was brief—a matter of less than ten years before the revolution was defeated—it offers a better glimpse than any other of what socialism could look like.

Because of this, the Russian Revolution has been the subject of countless lies and slanders. Chief among them is the idea that the 1917 revolution was a coup, organized by the master manipulators Lenin and Trotsky. Nothing could be further from the truth. The seeds of the revolution lay in the mass hatred of Russia's Tsar Nicholas II—and the misery of poverty and war that he presided over. The Russian Revolution began in February 1917 with nearly spontaneous demonstrations to commemorate International Working Women's Day. These spread dramatically in just a few days, until the capital of Petrograd was paralyzed and the tsar toppled.

Far from being a coup, the revolution depended on mass action—on thousands of confrontations like the one described by Trotsky in his *History of the Russian Revolution* between a crowd of workers and the Cossacks, the most brutal and feared unit of the tsar's army:

The workers at the Erikson, one of the foremost mills in the Vyborg district, after a morning meeting, came out on the Sampsonievsky Prospect, a whole mass, 2,500 of them, and in a narrow place ran into the Cossacks. Cutting their way with the breasts of their horses, the officers first charged through the crowd. Behind them, filling the whole width of the Prospect, galloped the Cossacks. Decisive moment! But the horsemen, cautiously, in a long ribbon, rode through the corridor just made by the officers. "Some of them smiled," Kayurov recalls, "and one of them gave the workers a good wink." This wink was not without meaning. The workers were emboldened with a friendly, not hostile, kind of assurance, and slightly infected the Cossacks with it. The one who winked found imitators. In spite of renewed efforts from the officers, the Cossacks, without openly breaking discipline, failed to force the crowd to disperse, but flowed through it in streams. This was repeated three or four times and brought the two sides even closer together. Individual Cossacks began to reply to the workers' questions and even to enter into momentary conversations with them. Of discipline, there remained but a thin transparent shell that threatened to break through any second. The officers hastened to separate their patrol from the workers, and, abandoning the idea of dispersing them, lined the Cossacks out across the street as a barrier to prevent the demonstrators from getting to the [center of the city]. But even this did not help: Standing stock-still in perfect discipline, the Cossacks did not hinder the workers from "diving" under their horses. The revolution does not choose its paths: it made its first steps toward victory under the belly of a Cossack's horse.

If Lenin and Trotsky and the Bolshevik Party they led ended up as leaders of the new workers' state, it was because they earned that position. The Bolsheviks eventually became a majority of the representatives to the soviets, the workers' councils. At the time, no one with any knowledge of the situation questioned this mass support. As Martov, a prominent opponent of the Bolsheviks, wrote, "Understand, please, what we have before us after all is a victorious uprising of the proletariat—almost the entire proletariat supports Lenin and expects its social liberation from the uprising." Even the final act of the revolution—the armed insurrection in October, in which workers took power from the capitalist government left behind after the tsar—was carried out with a minimum of resistance and violence.

The popular character of the Russian Revolution is also clear from looking at its initial accomplishments. The revolution put an end to Russia's participation in the First World War—a slaughter that left millions of workers dead in a conflict over which major powers would dominate the globe. Russia's entry into the war had been accompanied by a wave of patriotic frenzy, but masses of Russians came to reject the slaughter through bitter experience. The soldiers that the tsar depended on to defend his rule changed sides and joined the revolution— a decisive step in Russia, as it has been in all revolutions.

The Russian Revolution also dismantled the tsar's empire— what Lenin called a "prison-house" of nations that suffered for years under tsarist tyranny. These nations were given the unconditional right to self-determination. The tsar had used the most vicious anti-Semitism to prop up his rule—after the revolution, Jews led the workers' councils in Russia's two biggest cities. Laws outlawing homosexuality were repealed. Abortion was legalized and made available on demand. And the revolution started to remove the age-old burden of "women's work" in the family by organizing socialized child care and communal kitchens and laundries.

But just listing the proclamations doesn't do justice to the reality of workers' power. Russia was a society in the process of being remade from the bottom up. In the factories, workers began to take charge of production. The country's vast peasantry took over the land of the big landowners. In city neighborhoods, people organized all sorts of communal services. In general, decisions about the whole of society became decisions that the whole of society played a part in making. Russia became a cauldron of discussion—where the ideas of all were part of a debate about what to do. The memories of socialists who lived through the revolution are dominated by this sense of people's horizons opening up. As Krupskaya, a veteran of the Bolshevik Party and Lenin's wife, described it:

> The streets in those days presented a curious spectacle: everywhere people stood about in knots, arguing heatedly and discussing the latest events. I used to mingle with the crowd and listen. These street meetings were so interesting that it once took me three hours to walk from Shirokaya Street to the Krzesinska Mansion. The house in which we lived overlooked a courtyard, and even here, if you opened the window at night, you could hear a heated dispute. A soldier would be sitting there, and he always had an audience— usually some of the cooks or housemaids from next door, or some young people. An hour after midnight, you could catch snatches of talk—"Bolsheviks, Mensheviks ..." At three in the morning, "Milyukov, Bolsheviks ..." At five—still the same street-corner-meeting talk, politics, etc. Petrograd's white nights are always associated in my mind now with those all-night political disputes.

The tragedy is that workers' power survived for only a short time in Russia. In the years that followed 1917, the world's major powers, including the United States, organized an invasion force that fought alongside the dregs of tsarist society—ex-generals, aristocrats, and assorted hangers-on— in a civil war against the new workers' state. The revolution survived this assault, but at a terrible price. By 1922, as a result of the civil war, famine stalked Russia, and the working class—the class that made the Russian Revolution—was decimated. The basic element necessary for socialism to survive— abundance, rather than scarcity—was crushed.

Neither Lenin nor any other leader of the Russian Revolution had any illusion that a workers' state could survive this barbarism without the support of revolutions in more advanced countries. The Russian revolutionaries believed that the international struggle for socialism could be started in Russia—but that it could only be finished after an international socialist revolution. A wave of upheavals *did* sweep across Europe following the Russian Revolution and the end of the First World War, toppling monarchies in Germany and the Austro-Hungarian empire and shaking many other societies. But workers didn't succeed in taking power anywhere else for any length of time. So the Russian Revolution was left isolated.

In these desperate circumstances, Russia's shattered working class couldn't exercise power through workers' councils. More and more, decisions were made by a group of state bureaucrats. At first, the aim was to keep the workers' state alive until help came in the form of international revolution. But eventually, as the hope of revolution abroad faded, the leading figure in the bureaucracy, Joseph Stalin, and his allies began to eliminate any and all opposition to their rule—and started making decisions on the basis of how best to protect and increase their own power. Though continuing to use the rhetoric of socialism, they began to take back every gain won in the revolution—without exception. The soviets became rubber stamps for the decisions of the regime. The tsar's empire was rebuilt.

This counterrevolution wasn't carried out without opposition. In particular, Leon Trotsky led the struggle to defend socialist principles. To finally consolidate power, Stalin had to murder or hound into exile every single surviving leader of the 1917 revolution. Russia under Stalin became the opposite of the workers' state of 1917. Though they mouthed socialist phrases, Stalin and the thugs who followed him ran a dictatorship in which workers were every bit as exploited as in Western-style capitalist countries.

Sadly, many people associate socialism with Stalin's tyranny. That's certainly what supporters of capitalism encourage us to believe. After all, what better argument could there be against socialism than the idea that any attempt to win change is doomed to produce another Stalin? But Stalin's triumph in Russia wasn't inevitable. It was the result of a workers' revolution left isolated in a sea of capitalism—strangled until it was finally defeated.

Moreover, none of the slanders can erase what was accomplished by the revolution in Russia—history's most radical experiment so far in workers' democracy.

The Russian Revolution took place a century ago in the most backward country in Europe. We're obviously in a far better position today—something made plain by the examples of workers' struggles since 1917. The history of the twentieth century is filled with social explosions in which the struggles of workers took center stage. From Spain, France, and Portugal in Europe, to Iran in the Middle East, to Chile in South America, to Hungry and Poland under the thumb of the former Stalinist dictatorships in Eastern Europe, these upheavals—along with dozens of others—showed the power of workers to challenge the status quo and pose an alternative.

Though they failed to establish socialism, these revolutionary upheavals brought the mass of the population to life. And that is what socialism is about—a society created by the vast majority and organized around the priorities decided on by that majority. As the British author of children's books Arthur Ransome wrote of the new world he witnessed in revolutionary Russia:

> We have seen the flight of the young eagles. Nothing can destroy that fact, even if, later in the day, the eagles fall to earth one by one, with broken wings ... These men who have made the Soviet government in Russia, if they must fail, will fail with clean shields and clean hearts, having striven for an ideal which will live beyond them. Even if they fail, they will nonetheless have written a page of history more daring than any other which I can remember in the history of humanity.

CHAPTER SEVEN

Socialism, the Struggle, and You

"Every time I think about money, I shut down, because there is none." A lot of people feel like Tammy Linville. As of the end of 2009, the 29-year-old resident of Louisville, Kentucky, had been out of work for eighteen months, since losing her job as a clerical worker at the Census Bureau. Her partner was working—at a nearby Ford plant—but he wasn't getting full-time hours. The couple has two children, and Tammy told a *New York Times* reporter that she'd started "saving quarters for diapers." She said she suffered from panic attacks, brought on by the ever-present fear: "I just don't know what we're going to do."

So many millions of people in the United States have the same fear. By the end of 2009, more than one in every six adults shared the same fate as Tammy and her partner—they were out of a job or working part time because they couldn't find a full-time position. The effects of the crisis are so severe that they're hard to really grasp. According to one study by the Center for Economic and Policy Research, the Great Recession will ultimately cost U.S. workers more than $1 trillion in lost wages and salaries.

Around the world, as the twenty-first century rolls on, conditions are far more desperate for much larger numbers of people, and the threat of war and environmental disaster looms over all of us. Something different—an alternative to the status quo—is desperately needed.

The outlines of this grim situation were clear in late 2008. Nevertheless, many millions of people in the United States, not to mention around the world, looked to the future with a sense of hope. After eight long, corrupt, and violent years, the reign of George W. Bush was coming to an end. Not only that, but the new president seemed to promise a change in the way business gets done in Washington.

Barack Obama's journey from "Yes we can" to "No we won't" has been a bitter disappointment to his supporters. And it's not because most people were expecting miracles, either. The worst part isn't even that Obama failed to deliver on so many questions, but that he didn't really *try* to deliver—because he was never committed to what he promised in the first place. Rather than fight for change on the issues that concerned his core supporters, Barack Obama has proved to be a defender of the status quo.

Author Naomi Klein spoke for many people in an article written after the disastrous Copenhagen climate summit in late 2009: "I understand all the arguments about not promising what he can't deliver, about the dysfunction of the U.S. Senate, about the art of the possible. But spare me the lecture about how little power poor Obama has. No president since FDR has been handed as many opportunities to transform the U.S. into something that doesn't threaten the stability of life on this planet. He has refused to use each and every one of them."

It's a basic fact of life about politics under capitalism: If political leaders, don't feel pressure from below, they yield to the ever-present pressure from above—from Wall Street, from Corporate America, from the political and military establishment. Anyone who wants the kind of change that Obama's presidency seemed to promise is going to have to do something about it.

"Men may not get all they pay for in this world, but they most certainly pay for all they get," Frederick Douglass said. "If we are ever to get free from the oppressions and wrongs heaped upon us, we must pay for their removal."

So where do we start? It's worth looking at a political movement from the first year of the Obama presidency—the rise of the new civil rights struggle for LGBT equality—that took shape largely outside the confines of mainstream politics and the liberal organizations shaped by that system.

It started with a setback—the passage of Proposition 8 in California, which stripped same-sex couples of the right to marry won previously through a state Supreme Court decision. Angry supporters of equal marriage rights took to the streets the night of the election, then the next night, and the next, continuing each day for the rest of the week. The protests spread from big California cities to smaller ones, then across the state, and to cities across the country. Less than two weeks after the election, a call for a national day of action on a newly created Web site led to demonstrations in three hundred cities.

Out of the protests and marches, new organizations formed, literally overnight in some cases, drawing in people with little or no experience in activist politics but with priceless enthusiasm for organizing. These forces became the backbone for the National Equality March in October 2009, a mobilization built with meager resources that brought more than 200,000 people to Washington D.C., and set its sights on full equality for LGBT people in all matters governed by civil law, in all fifty states.

Among Democrats, the National Equality March was dismissed as "a waste of time at best," as Congressman Barney Frank told a reporter a few days before. "The only thing they're going to be putting pressure on is the grass." Mainstream LGBT organizations like the Human Rights Campaign took a similar, if less publicly contemptuous, attitude, offering token support only at the last minute.

This is typical behavior for the inhabitants of insider Washington. The same people insisted in 2006 that no progress could be made on repealing the Defense of Marriage Act or "don't ask, don't tell" in the military until the Democrats took back Congress—and then in 2008, until a Democrat was in the White House. Now, with Obama in the Oval Office and Democrats with big majorities in both houses of Congress, they still called for patience.

The National Equality March was an important step past this "wait, not yet" attitude. The LGBT equality movement has a long road ahead of it. There will be defeats as well as victories, and ebbs and flows in activity. But the point is that its grassroots strength shows a different vision and strategy that other movements for change badly need.

The LGBT civil rights movement illustrates something else, too—what individuals do is important. Without the handfuls of people—many of them without experience in activism—who took the initiative to call demonstrations on and after Election Day, the prevailing response to Prop 8 might have been demoralization. Without the individuals and organizations that adopted the call for a national mobilization as their own and did the hard work of organizing to turn people out, Barney Frank's sneering comments would have been the last word on the National Equality March.

What we do—or don't do—matters. In this sense, politics isn't something that happens only in Washington. It doesn't just belong to the politicians or media commentators, or to union leaders and heads of civil rights and liberal organizations. Politics belongs to all of us—because how we answer political questions, and how we act on those answers, helps decide what happens in society.

One of the chief characteristics of recent decades has been a widespread frustration and bitterness on all kinds of political questions in the United States—from America's wars, to inequality and oppression, to deteriorating living standards for working people. But that bitterness hasn't been matched by as high a level of struggle and political mobilization. By the last years of his presidency, George Bush's war on Iraq was strongly opposed by a majority of the population—but the multibillion-dollar-war-spending bills would pass Congress with barely token Democratic opposition, and antiwar demonstrations were few and far between. The bailout of the Wall Street banksters infuriated overwhelming numbers of people, but the labor movement didn't do anything beyond a few symbolic protests.

There's no shortcut for bridging the gap between anger and action. Social and political movements with the kind of support and broad-based mobilization necessary to be an alternative to the mainstream establishment—with the power to really change the status quo, like the civil rights movement, for example—don't spring to life fully formed. The history of every past struggle for freedom and justice shows that such movements have to be built, step by step.

There *are* high points in the struggle—like the Montgomery Bus Boycott, which began when Rosa Parks was arrested in December 1955 for refusing to give up her seat to a white man. But we also should remember the moments before the high points, when Rosa Parks built the local NAACP chapter in Montgomery, when she attended meetings at the Highlander Folk School in Tennessee to discuss the future of the struggle, when she participated in protests against segregation that didn't result in a citywide revolt by the African American population. Those moments laid the basis for the high points to come.

In a system based on inequality and injustice, there are issues in every corner of society that need to be organized around. But whether there is action—whether the protests get called, whether the planning meetings are organized, whether the buses to Washington get lined up and the signs get made—depends on what people decide to do about it.

The Case for Socialist Organization

When the high points of struggle do come, things can change very quickly. People's ideas especially—about what's wrong, what can be done, whether something can be done—can shift fast. By taking action for even limited demands, people begin to learn who their allies are, what they're up against, what tactics work and don't work in advancing their cause.

But ideas don't change all at once. In any movement, there are always some people who are more determined to confront the employers or the political powers that be, more committed to standing up for the oppressed, more confident about fighting for a political alternative. Nor do people stay the same. Consciousness changes under the impact of real events—victories and defeats in struggle, the overall political climate, and so on—going both forward and backward.

So at every step of the way, there are different ideas about what to do about any political issue. Some people will see the need to take action or to make the link to other political issues. Others will argue that protesting makes matters worse. Still others will have ideas about various ways to build beyond the strategies that have been tried before. The outcome of these discussions and debates shapes the outcome of the struggle.

This is one way that the participation of socialists, who can express the lessons of past struggles and suggest a way forward, can be very important. Socialists who are part of an organization can share their experiences and come to a common understanding about what can be done, whether in a workplace or a community or at a school. The strength of such an organization is in the range of experiences and the political understanding of all its members, which can then carry over into whatever political activity they're involved in.

None of that would be of any use to a political party like the Democrats. The Democratic Party exists for one reason—to get Democrats elected to office. For that, it needs its supporters to help raise money and vote once or twice every few years—and nothing more, by and large. The organization of the party is bent to these ends. Its supporters at the grass roots have no mechanism to influence the leadership above them. In other words, the Democratic Party is utterly undemocratic.

Socialists have very different goals, so our political organization will have to look very different. We need socialists active not every few years but every day. We need socialists in every workplace, responding to grievances and political questions. We need socialists in every neighborhood to take up the issues of housing and schools and police violence. We need socialists on campuses organizing speakouts and protests. We need socialists in every corner of society inhabited by working people, and we need these socialists working nonstop, organizing struggle, carrying on political discussions, and educating themselves and others.

To achieve this, a revolutionary socialist organization has to be much more democratic than other political organizations under capitalism. We need to bring together the experiences of everyone who takes part, as well as those passed down to us from the history of past struggles, and make them part of a common basis for everyone to organize around. That means debate and discussion throughout the organization, and a structure that holds those elected to leadership positions accountable.

But a socialist organization has to be centralized as well—to be prepared to act together on the basis of those discussions and the democratic decisions that come out of them. If there's no centralism to hold members accountable for carrying out the decisions of the majority, then the democratic procedures for making those decisions are ultimately pointless.

This question of organization is one of the most controversial ones for the socialist movement. The very idea that socialists might be part of an organization is regarded with suspicion and downright hostility, not only by the right, but also many on the left. One reason is the enduring effects of Stalinism, which turned supposedly communist parties in the USSR and around the world into top-down apparatuses—in other words, all centralism and no democracy.

But another reason runs deeper. Particularly among those new to the left, there's often an instinctive reaction against the idea that anyone in the movement should be held accountable to a decision they disagree with, even if it's a decision of the majority. After all, goes the argument, if we're fighting for a new world based on freedom, why shouldn't our movement reflect that in the here and now? Shouldn't people be free to act in whatever way they think is best?

The problem is that we don't live in a world of freedom today—and the other side is organized to keep it that way.

The ruling class under capitalism presides over a highly structured and stratified system designed to perpetuate exploitation and oppression. For all the talk of the free market, individual businesses are anything but democratic. The ruling class organizes and distributes its political propaganda through the mainstream mass media and the education system. It can respond to resistance with a rigidly organized and disciplined police force and army. And it coordinates the response of all its institutions in a crisis—think of how the executives who presided over the Wall Street crash of 2008 suddenly showed up in the federal government's Treasury Department to oversee the bailout.

Because the ruling class is a tiny minority of society, it couldn't rule without this organization. So any attempt to challenge that rule means challenging its organization. This requires some level of symmetry—that is, organization on our side to match up to the organization on their side. If their mass media carries out a slander campaign to smear our unions, we need an equally organized response—our own newspapers and magazines and Web sites to defend the movement and put forward our vision for change. If their police force is ordered to crack down on protests, we need a response—an organized strategy, relying on the strength of our much greater numbers, to defend our ranks against state violence and repression.

These elements of organization for our side exist at the most basic level in practically every struggle, no matter how small. Even a modest speakout needs to be planned and advertised; a petition has to be written, distributed, and collected; any resistance in a workplace needs to get support from coworkers—they all require people working together to some degree.

When you look at rebellions that seem to erupt out of nowhere, the elements of organization aren't always obvious from the outside. But to the participants, it's another story. Take, for example, the mobilization of the barrios in Venezuela after the April 2002 coup attempt against President Hugo Chávez. Chávez had already been kidnapped and flown out of the country on a military plane and a new coup government installed in office when the poor residents of Caracas streamed into the city center. The Chávista revolt shook the elite, and sections of the military lost their nerve—the coup regime collapsed, and Chávez returned to Venezuela in triumph.

Most of the descriptions of the crucial demonstrations that turned the tide described them as spontaneous. But to the people who took part in them, they were a conscious act that required very determined organizing in a tense and rapidly developing situation—recognizing what the coup represented, getting others to participate, helping people to overcome their fears, finding the best ways to put pressure on the elite.

Of course, some political events are more organized than others—and some periods in any struggle demand a higher level of organization. The history of past struggles shows the importance of both action *and* organization—in differing proportions, depending on the circumstances. In the French Revolution of 1789, for example, no one drew up a plan to have a rebellion in Paris that would topple the king. It wasn't necessary to hold a discussion about whether the Bastille prison would be a good rallying point for the Parisian masses. Likewise, in Russia in February 1917, no socialist organization set the date for a wave of strikes and street battles to overthrow the tsar. In those cases, the accumulated hatred for the tyranny of the old regime was enough to set the process in motion.

But with the king or the tsar out of the way, what then? The new circumstances presented political challenges that couldn't be solved purely through organization in action. Political organization, built around a vision of what came next in the struggle, was needed. How far should the revolution go? What was needed to make sure the king or tsarism never came back? The answers to these questions were decided ultimately by a test of the organization of the rival sides—the revolutionary Jacobins versus the more moderate Gironde in France; the Bolsheviks versus the Mensheviks in 1917 Russia.

Organization like this doesn't emerge overnight—it has to be built. This is particularly true of socialist organization, which aims to be part of many movements against oppression and exploitation and unite them in a wider struggle for socialism. Such an organization has to be built up over time, contributing what it can to every fight it's involved in, providing the living link between various movements, absorbing the experiences of various struggles, and testing its ideas against reality. Its members have to learn the ideas and history of socialism and engage in a constant discussion about their meaning today in order to be ready to offer a way forward in future struggles.

So this is the further case for socialism—why you should be a socialist, not just in thought, but in deed, as part of the socialist movement. We need many more socialists in that movement if we want to play a positive role in the struggles of today and put forward our alternative to capitalism.

But something else is true as well: You need us. If you want to change society, you can't do it alone. As individuals on our own, we can't accomplish much—not even with the best grasp of what's wrong with the world and how it could be different. But as part of an organization committed to speaking out for every struggle for justice, we can make a difference.

The participation of socialists in many struggles is the source of a lot of bluster when right-wingers uncover this not-so-hidden fact. They think they've exposed a secret plot—the teacher opposed to the anti-union charter school invasion in her city, who also marched against the Israeli onslaught against Gaza and once wrote a letter to the editor in favor of socialized medicine. She probably even recycles!

Our determination to fight against all instances of oppression and injustice isn't some dark secret. It's a point of pride. You'll find socialists organizing for LGBT equality, participating in sit-ins and occupations against tuition hikes and budget cuts on college campuses, fighting in workplaces for union rights, defending the victims of racism caught up in the criminal injustice system, demonstrating against war and in solidarity with people struggling for liberation around the world.

Who wouldn't be proud to be part of a movement whose members protest the wretched American health care system in the morning, walk a picket line with strikers in the afternoon, and attend a forum on how to save the environment in the evening? Why shouldn't activists dedicated to organizing today want to learn the history of the working-class movement of the past—and see their own efforts as part of a tradition of struggle for a better world?

Here's our answer to any windbag who "discovers" the diabolical socialist plot to be a part of as many efforts to make the world a better place as possible: We only wish there were more of us, and more of those efforts. And we want to correct these shortcomings as quickly as possible.

One question that socialists *don't* have to answer is how to stay busy. There are struggles that need to be organized and championed everywhere in our society. By doing so, we can make a difference right now, and show how the day-to-day fights of the present are part of a bigger struggle for fundamental change. As Marx and Engels put it more than 150 years ago: "The Communists fight for the attainment of the immediate aims, for the enforcement of the momentary interests of the working class; but in the movement of the present, they also represent and take care of the future of that movement."

A World to Win

We live in an ugly and frightening world—the world of capitalism, with its poverty and famine and environmental destruction and war. For shockingly large numbers of people, just surviving from day to day is incredibly difficult. For the rest of the vast majority, the struggle to get by leaves little time for what we really care about.

But according to the conventional wisdom, this is inevitable.

It may not be a perfect world, we're told, but that's a pipe dream anyway. This is the best we can do—and the best we can hope for in the future is to stop things from getting worse.

John Lloyd, a one-time radical and now correspondent for the *Financial Times*, wrote an article in 2009—a review of a short book about socialism, in fact—in which he warned against attempting to change the world. Better, Lloyd wrote, to accept that we live in "a good enough society. A liberal democracy with a strong social base is the best we can do, and at least for now, our governments' central duty is to try to keep it that way. For this may be as good as it gets."

This? As good as it gets? A world in which six million children die of malnutrition every year is as good as it gets? The carnage in Iraq and Afghanistan and countries around the globe is as good as it gets? Unemployment and home foreclosures ravaging even wealthier societies? A society plagued by racism and sexism and bigotry? A planet threatened by ecological disaster?

What a telling indictment of capitalism that its defenders think this is the best we can do—still more that they conjure up justifications for why poverty is natural, why inequality is beneficial to everyone, why war is just, why human beings are incapable of making a world organized around solidarity and freedom.

There may be a long struggle ahead of us to make a new society. But if you join the socialists, at least you'll never again have to be satisfied with these shameful excuses.

Actually, millions of people reject this kind of complacency in the face of society's failures. They may not see themselves as rebels or have an alternative in mind. They may voice their discontent to a few friends or coworkers, or they may save it for cursing at Glenn Beck and Lou Dobbs on TV. Some create works of art that imagine different worlds. But they don't accept that this world is as good as it gets, and that nothing can be done about it. And some of them will put that sentiment into action— to get involved, whether on their own behalf or someone else's.

At times, the power of our rulers may seem too great to be challenged on even a single issue, much less the many that socialists care about. But it should be remembered that African Americans feared the same about the murderous racists who ruled over the U.S. South during Jim Crow segregation. The people of Eastern Europe believed that the tyrants who oppressed them were too powerful to be stopped. So did Blacks under South Africa's apartheid system, or the workers of Petrograd in tsarist Russia. So has every victim of the oppressors throughout history.

No one knows beforehand when the high points of struggle will happen, but we do know that they're shaped by the organizing that came before. Without the Rosa Parks and Fannie Lou Hamers, without the Eugene Debses and Elizabeth Gurley Flynns, without Frederick Douglass and John Brown and Wendell Phillips—without the whole long list of socialists and radicals and rebels whose names we remember, and the many hundreds and thousands we don't—our history would be very different. The struggle for a better world turned on their decision not to wait and see what others did. Instead, they took a stand.

"To be a socialist in the United States," author Mike Davis told PBS's Bill Moyers, "is ... really to stand in the shadow [of an] immense history of radicalism and labor, but with a responsibility to ensure its regeneration." That's the challenge facing us: To present the socialist alternative to capitalism and make it a part of all the movements for change—to capture the spirit of resistance from the rich history of the working-class movement and bring it to life in the struggles of today.

We live in a world where it's possible to put an end to war and famine and poverty forever. Why should we ever accept that what we have now is the best we can do? Socialists want to build a society free of all oppression, built on the principles of solidarity and democracy, where we control our own lives. That's a world worth fighting for.

Eugene V. Debs and the Idea of Socialism

We are always in need of radicals who are also lovable, and so we would do well to remember Eugene Victor Debs. Ninety years ago, and the time the Progressive was born, Debs was nationally famous as leader of the Socialist Party, and the poet James Whitcomb Riley wrote of him:

> As warm a heart as ever beat
> Betwixt here and the Judgment Seat.

Debs was what every socialist or anarchist or radical should be: fierce in his convictions, kind and compassionate in his personal relations. Sam Moore, a fellow inmate of the Atlanta penitentiary, where Debs was imprisoned for opposing the First World War, remembered how he felt as Debs was about to be released on Christmas Day, 1921:

> As miserable as I was, I would defy fate with all its cruelty as long as Debs held my hand, and I was the most miserably happiest man on Earth when I knew he was going home Christmas.

Howard Zinn was the author of *A People's History of the United States: 1492–Present*. This article first appeared in the *Progressive* in January 1999, and is reprinted here with permission from both the author and the magazine.

Debs had won the hearts of his fellow prisoners in Atlanta. He had fought for them in a hundred ways and refused any special privileges for himself. On the day of his release, the warden ignored prison regulations and opened every cellblock to allow more than two thousand inmates to gather in front of the main jail building to say goodbye to Eugene Debs. As he started down the walkway from the prison, a roar went up and he turned, tears streaming down his face, and stretched out his arms to the other prisoners.

This was not his first prison experience. In 1894, not yet a socialist but an organizer for the American Railway Union, he had led a nationwide boycott of the railroads in support of the striking workers at the Pullman Palace Car Company. They tied up the railroad system, burned hundreds of railway cars, and were met with the full force of the capitalist state: Attorney General Richard Olney, a former railroad lawyer, got a court injunction to prohibit blocking trains. President Cleveland called out the army, which used bayonets and rifle fire on a crowd of five thousand strike sympathizers in Chicago. Seven hundred were arrested. Thirteen were shot to death.

Debs was jailed for violating an injunction prohibiting him from doing or saying anything to carry on the strike. In court, he denied he was a socialist, but during his six months in prison he read socialist literature, and the events of the strike took on a deeper meaning. He wrote later:

> I was to be baptized in socialism in the roar of conflict. In the gleam of every bayonet and the flash of every rifle the class struggle was revealed.

From then on, Debs devoted his life to the cause of working people and the dream of a socialist society. He stood on the platform with Mother Jones and Big Bill Haywood in 1905 at the founding convention of the Industrial Workers of the World. He was a magnificent speaker, his long body leaning forward from the podium, his arm raised dramatically. Thousands came to hear him talk all over the country.

With the outbreak of war in Europe in 1914 and the buildup of war fever against Germany, some socialists succumbed to the talk of "preparedness," but Debs was adamantly opposed. When President Wilson and Congress brought the nation into the war in 1917, speech was no longer free. The Espionage Act made it a crime to say anything that would discourage enlistment in the armed forces.

Soon, close to one thousand people were in prison for protesting the war. The producer of a movie called *The Spirit of '76*, about the American Revolution, was sentenced to ten years in prison for promoting anti-British feeling at a time when England and the United States were allies. The case was officially labeled *The U.S. v. The Spirit of '76*.

Debs made a speech in Canton, Ohio, in support of the men and women in jail for opposing the war. He told his listeners:

Wars throughout history have been waged for conquest and plunder. And that is war, in a nutshell. The master class has always declared the wars; the subject class has always fought the battles.

He was found guilty and sentenced to ten years in prison by a judge who denounced those "who would strike the sword from the hand of the nation while she is engaged in defending herself against a foreign and brutal power."

In court, Debs refused to call any witnesses, declaring: "I have been accused of obstructing the war. I admit it. I abhor war. I would oppose war if I stood alone." Before sentencing, Debs spoke to judge and jury, uttering perhaps his most famous words. I was in his hometown of Terre Haute, Indiana, recently, among two hundred people gathered to honor his memory, and we began the evening by reciting those words—words that moved me deeply when I first read them and move me deeply still:

> While there is a lower class, I am in it. While there is a criminal element, I am of it. While there is a soul in prison, I am not free.

The "liberal" Oliver Wendell Holmes, speaking for a unanimous Supreme Court, upheld the verdict, on the ground that Debs's speech was intended to obstruct military recruiting. When the war was over, the "liberal" Woodrow Wilson turned down his attorney general's recommendation that Debs be released, even though he was sixty-five and in poor health. Debs was in prison for thirty-two months. Finally, in 1921, the Republican Warren Harding ordered him freed on Christmas Day.

Today, when capitalism, "the free market," and "private enterprise" are being hailed as triumphant in the world, it is a good time to remember Debs and to rekindle the idea of socialism.

To see the disintegration of the Soviet Union as a sign of the failure of socialism is to mistake the monstrous tyranny created by Stalin for the vision of an egalitarian and democratic society that has inspired enormous numbers of people all over the world. Indeed, the removal of the Soviet Union as the false surrogate for the idea of socialism creates a great opportunity. We can now reintroduce genuine socialism to a world feeling the sickness of capitalism—its nationalist hatreds, its perpetual warfare, riches for a small number of people in a small number of countries, and hunger, homelessness, insecurity for everyone else.

Here in the United States we should recall that enthusiasm for socialism—production for use instead of profit, economic and social equality, solidarity with our brothers and sisters all over the world—was at its height before the Soviet Union came into being.

In the era of Debs, the first seventeen years of the twentieth century—until war created an opportunity to crush the movement—millions of Americans declared their adherence to the principles of socialism. Those were years of bitter labor struggles, the great walkouts of women garment workers in New York, the victorious multi-ethnic strike of textile workers in Lawrence, Massachusetts, the unbelievable courage of coal miners in Colorado, defying the power and wealth of the Rockefellers. The I.W.W. was born—revolutionary, militant, demanding "one big union" for everyone, skilled and unskilled, black and white, men and women, native-born and foreign-born.

More than a million people read Appeal to Reason and other socialist newspapers. In proportion to population, it would be as if today more than three million Americans read a socialist press. The party had 100,000 members, and 1,200 office-holders in 340 municipalities. Socialism was especially strong in the Southwest, among tenant farmers, railroad workers, coal miners, lumberjacks. Oklahoma had 12,000 dues-paying members in 1914 and more than one hundred socialists in local offices. It was the home of the fiery Kate Richards O'Hare. Jailed for opposing the war, she once hurled a book through the skylight to bring fresh air into the foul-smelling jail block, bringing cheers from her fellow inmates.

The point of recalling all this is to remind us of the powerful appeal of the socialist idea to people alienated from the political system and aware of the growing stark disparities in income and wealth—as so many Americans are today. The word itself—"socialism"—may still carry the distortions of recent experience in bad places usurping the name. But anyone who goes around the country, or reads carefully the public opinion surveys over the past decade, can see that huge numbers of Americans agree on what should be the fundamental elements of a decent society: guaranteed food, housing, medical care for everyone; bread and butter as better guarantees of "national security" than guns and bombs; democratic control of corporate power; equal rights for all races, genders, and sexual orientations; a recognition of the rights of immigrants as the unrecognized counterparts of our parents and grandparents; the rejection of war and violence as solutions for tyranny and injustice.

There are people fearful of the word, all along the political spectrum. What is important, I think, is not the word, but a determination to hold up before a troubled public those ideas that are both bold and inviting—the more bold, the more inviting. That's what remembering Debs and the socialist idea can do for us.

Acknowledgments

This is the third edition of *The Case for Socialism*. Both new versions started out as an "updated edition" and gradually transmogrified into "completely revised and updated." It would be more accurate to say: "Completely revised and updated, also inexcusably longer and took-for*ever*-for-him-to-finish edition." I want to thank Ahmed Shawki, Anthony Arnove, and Julie Fain at Haymarket Books for encouraging me to try again and teaching me so much over the years.

I got a lot of help from people who took the time to read all or parts of the book; many, many thanks to Lance Selfa, Todd Chretien, Marlene Martin, Dao Tran, Brian Jones, Josh On, and Rachel Cohen for their suggestions, not to mention the mistakes they caught.

I'm also heavily indebted to the people who lend their talents to SocialistWorker.org and *Socialist Worker* newspaper. In particular, the core staff of Lee Sustar, Elizabeth Schulte, Eric Ruder, Nicole Colson, and David Whitehouse has contributed enormously to my knowledge and understanding through our years of working together. A lot of what they've said and wrote found its way into these pages, as is true for other *SW* writers.

This book begins from the premise that if you want to see change in society, you have to be part of the struggle. I've been a member of the International Socialist Organization for more than twenty-five years, and everything in this book is the result of that involvement. In addition to the people I've mentioned already, I have to thank Sharon Smith, Paul D'Amato, Bill Roberts, Sherry Wolf, Jennifer Roesch, Joel Geier, Ashley Smith, Phil Gasper, Dave Zirin, Shaun Harkin, and Adam Turl for everything they've contributed to this book.

That's not even close to listing the many more people who deserve thanks from me, if only I had the space and a better memory. Without everything I've learned from them in political discussions and as part of movements for change, there wouldn't be much to this book—some quotes from Springsteen and Clash songs, maybe.

Speaking of Springsteen, I also wanted to thank whoever thought of music, or this book would have *never* gotten finished.

And then there's Daisy Maass and Marlene Martin, who endured many days and nights of crankiness and distraction. I hope they like this book, and find in it the spirit and life that I love in them.

What Else to Read

If you noticed that this book doesn't have footnotes, you're not alone. I've gotten complaints about previous editions that I didn't cite my sources. Sorry, I'm a journalist, and that's the writing style I used for this book. But that doesn't mean there aren't sources for every fact in it. If you see a statistic or quote, and you're curious about where I found it, I'll go through my notes and track down the source if you e-mail me at maass@socialistworker.org.

As for where to learn more about the ideas in this book, I think the place to start is **SocialistWorker.org**, a now daily Web site connected to *Socialist Worker* newspaper. Since going daily in 2008, the *SW* Web site has expanded to include not only all the writers who filled the pages of the newspaper in the past, but a range of voices from the U.S. and international left. You'll find a strong analysis of politics in the United States and around the world, plus articles about the history and ideas of the socialist tradition. But equally important, in my opinion, are the reports from struggles across the country—a view from the grassroots of what people are thinking and doing in the fight for a better world.

The *International Socialist Review* is one of the best left-wing journals around—a bimonthly source for facts and perspectives about contemporary political issues and discussions of historical and theoretical questions.

What books should you turn to next? Top on my list would be *The Meaning of Marxism* by Paul D'Amato. It's a wonderful introduction to the ideas that underlay the socialist tradition—starting with the writings of Karl Marx and his collaborator Frederick Engels and continuing with later Marxists. Paul has a great ability for making even complicated concepts easy to understand. But he also includes long passages from Marx and other Marxists that prove they aren't the dull and dense theorists they sometimes seem to be when academics write about them.

Haymarket Books has been publishing an excellent series of books that take up important political questions from the standpoint of socialist theory and the history of the struggle. These are must-reads: Ahmed Shawki's *Black Liberation and Socialism*, Sharon Smith's *Women and Socialism: Essays on Women's Liberation*, and Sherry Wolf's *Sexuality and Socialism: History, Politics, and Theory of LGBT Liberation*.

The single-best case for socialism was written more than 160 years ago by Karl Marx and Frederick Engels: *The Communist Manifesto*. A recent edition from Haymarket has an annotation of the *Manifesto* itself, plus a collection of related writings from Marx and Engels and excellent supplementary essays about Marxism's relevance today, all put together by Phil Gasper.

There are a lot of other well-known books and booklets from the Marxist tradition that should be read and reread, along with the *Manifesto*. SocialistWorker.org ran a series of articles introducing "Ten Socialist Classics," including writings by Marx, Engels, Rosa Luxemburg, V. I. Lenin, and Leon Trotsky. You can find the full list at: socialistworker.org/series/Ten-socialist-classics.

What we think about the world today depends on what we know and understand of the past—both how the rulers of society have ruled, and how those below them resisted. When it comes to understanding the U.S. working-class movement, Sharon Smith's *Subterranean Fire: A History of Working-Class Radicalism in the United States* is indispensable. The book does a wonderful job of both telling the hidden story of the American working class, and situating that history in U.S. politics and society overall. Likewise, Lance Selfa's *The Democrats: A Critical History* is an excellent analysis of the most important questions in American politics over the decades, through the lens of a history of the "party of the people."

This is just a starter list, so I won't go any further, except on one subject—the Russian Revolution, since it's so important to the socialist case. Your first book should be *Ten Days That Shook the World,* an eyewitness account by American journalist and socialist John Reed. Leon Trotsky's *History of the Russian Revolution* is more than 1,200 pages long, but every one is worth the read. Tony Cliff's multipart political biographies of *Lenin* and *Trotsky* are excellent guides to the ideas of these two revolutionary leaders, and Duncan Hallas's *The Comintern* looks at the impact of the revolution internationally. For understanding what happened to Russia after the revolution, check out ***Russia: From Workers' State to State Capitalism.***

Finally, in closing out this book, there are some socialists I want to remember.

A few months after I finished the last edition of this book in 2004, the British socialist and journalist Paul Foot died. Foot wrote several short books and pamphlets on socialism among several dozen others, including one called ***The Case for Socialism.*** I've borrowed (or, less charitably, stolen) heavily from them for many years, and continue to do so today. Foot was an electrifying speaker and the best journalist I ever read. Buy any book with his name on it. And if you want to become a writer, this is my advice: read a lot of Foot and another British socialist by the name of George Orwell; and try to write just like them.

At the end of 2009, Chris Harman, also a British socialist and member of the Socialist Workers Party, died suddenly. Harman was the author of many fine books on a vast array of topics, including the excellent introductory ***How Marxism Works.*** He wrote about so much that it's hard to single out one area, but I'd suggest ***A People's History of the World***, literally an attempt to apply Marxism to all of human history, from the first examples of settled societies thousands of years ago through to the international capitalist system today.

And now, as I'm finishing this edition, comes news of the death of Howard Zinn, whose article on Eugene V. Debs is included as an afterword here. Zinn was a unique figure—a historian who changed history. His books awakened millions of people to the violence and injustice at the core of American history, as well as the traditions of resistance that confronted them. And he participated in the most important struggles of the last half century, from the civil rights movement to antiwar struggles over several different decades and more. So, in the unlikely event that you don't have them yet, these should go on your reading list as well: *A People's History of the United States* and the companion volume of primary documents, edited with Anthony Arnove, *Voices of a People's History of the United States*.

Index

Also from Haymarket Books

The Bending Cross: A Biography of Eugene V. Debs
Ray Ginger, introduction by Mike Davis • Orator, organizer, self-taught scholar, presidential candidate, and prisoner, Eugene Debs' lifelong commitment to the fight for a better world is chronicled in this unparalleled biography by historian Ray Ginger. This moving story presents the definitive account of the life and legacy of the most eloquent spokesperson and leader of the U.S. labor and socialist movements. • ISBN 9781931859400

Black Liberation and Socialism
Ahmed Shawki • A sharp and insightful analysis of historic movements against racism in the United States—from the separatism of Marcus Garvey, to the militancy of Malcolm X and the Black Panther Party, to the eloquence of Martin Luther King Jr., and much more. • ISBN 9781931859264

Bolsheviks Come to Power
Alexander Rabinowitch • In this absorbing narrative, Alexander Rabinowitch refutes the Soviet myth that the party's triumph in the October Revolution was inevitable, as well as the long-held view of many Western historians that the Bolsheviks won primarily because of their unity, discipline, and responsiveness to Lenin's revolutionary leadership. Exploring the changing situation and aspirations of workers, soldiers, and Baltic fleet sailors in Petrograd, Rabinowitch's classic account reveals the critical link between the party's revolutionary tactics and the Petrograd masses. • ISBN 9780745322681

Breaking the Sound Barrier
Amy Goodman, Edited by Denis Moynihan • Amy Goodman, award-winning host of the daily internationally broadcast radio and television program *Democracy Now!*, breaks through the cor-

porate media's lies, sound bites, and silence in this wide-ranging new collection of articles. • ISBN 9781931859998

The Communist Manifesto: A Road Map to History's Most Important Political Document
Edited by Phil Gasper • This beautifully organized, fully annotated edition of *The Communist Manifesto* is complete with historical references and explication, additional related texts and a thorough glossary. • ISBN 9781931859257

The Democrats: A Critical History
Lance Selfa • Offering a broad historical perspective, Selfa shows how the Democratic Party has time and again betrayed the aspirations of ordinary people while pursuing an agenda favorable to Wall Street and U.S. imperial ambitions. • ISBN 9791931859554

The Forging of the American Empire: From the Revolution to Vietnam
Sidney Lens, foreword by Howard Zinn • *The Forging of the American Empire* tells the story of a nation that has conducted more than 160 wars and other military ventures while insisting that it loves peace. This comprehensive history of American imperialism punctures this myth once and for all by showing how the U.S., from the time it gained its own independence, has used every available means—political, economic, and military—to dominate other peoples. • ISBN 9780745321004

Independent Politics: The Green Party Strategy Debate
Edited by Howie Hawkins • Leading independent and Green Party activists ask: Can we break the two party stranglehold on U.S. politics? Ralph Nader, Peter Camejo, and other Green Party members and allies assess the 2000 and 2004 presidential elections, and debate strategy for how to build a challenge to the Republicans and an increasingly corporate Democratic Party. • ISBN 9781931859301

The Meaning of Marxism

Paul D'Amato • This book is a lively and accessible introduction to the ideas of Karl Marx, as well as other key Marxists, with historical and contemporary examples. *The Meaning of Marxism* shows that a "radical, fundamental transformation of existing society" is not only possible, but urgently necessary. • ISBN 9781931859295

No One is Illegal: Fighting Racism
and State Violence on the U.S.–Mexico Border

Mike Davis and Justin Akers-Chacón • *No One Is Illegal* debunks the leading ideas behind the often-violent right-wing backlash against immigrants, revealing deep roots in U.S. history. The authors also remember the long tradition of resistance among immigrants organizing in the factories and the fields, and chart a course toward justice and equality for immigrants in the U.S. • ISBN 9781931859356

Sexuality and Socialism:
History, Theory, and Politics of LGBT Liberation

Sherry Wolf • *Sexuality and Socialism* addresses many of the most challenging questions for those concerned with full equality for lesbian, gay, bisexual, and transgender (LGBT) people, and challenges myths about genes, gender, and sexuality. • ISBN 9781931859790

Subterranean Fire:
A History of Working-Class Radicalism in the United States

Sharon Smith • Workers in the U.S. have a rich tradition of fightback, which remains largely hidden. *Subterranean Fire* brings that history to light and reveals its lessons for today. • ISBN 9781931859233

Women and Socialism

Sharon Smith • Thirty years have passed since the heyday of the women's liberation struggle, yet women remain second-class citizens. Feminism has shifted steadily rightward since the 1960s. This collection of essays examines these issues from a Marxist perspective, badly needed today. • ISBN 9781931859110

About Haymarket Books

Haymarket Books is a nonprofit, progressive book distributor and publisher, a project of the Center for Economic Research and Social Change. We believe that activists need to take ideas, history, and politics into the many struggles for social justice today. Learning the lessons of past victories, as well as defeats, can arm a new generation of fighters for a better world. As Karl Marx said, "The philosophers have merely interpreted the world; the point, however, is to change it."

We take inspiration and courage from our namesakes, the Haymarket Martyrs, who gave their lives fighting for a better world. Their 1886 struggle for the eight-hour day, which gave us May Day, the international workers' holiday, reminds workers around the world that ordinary people can organize and struggle for their own liberation. These struggles continue today across the globe—struggles against oppression, exploitation, hunger, and poverty.

It was August Spies, one of the Martyrs targeted for being an immigrant and an anarchist, who predicted the battles being fought to this day. "If you think that by hanging us you can stamp out the labor movement," Spies told the judge, "then hang us. Here you will tread upon a spark, but here, and there, and behind you, and in front of you, and everywhere, the flames will blaze up. It is a subterranean fire. You cannot put it out. The ground is on fire upon which you stand."

We could not succeed in our publishing efforts without the generous financial support of our readers. Many people contribute to our project through the Haymarket Sustainers program, where donors receive free books in return for their monetary support. If you would like to be a part of this program, please contact us at info@haymarketbooks.org.

Shop our full catalogue online at www.haymarketbooks.org or call 773-583-7884.